SPIRIT SP[...]

"This is a book that has been long overdue and whose time has come! Salicrow shows her authentic self and her expertise in every word. She writes in a direct and easy-to-understand manner that makes you feel you are right there with her. *Spirit Speaker* is a detailed and all-inclusive guide for anyone who wishes to explore the skill or desires to learn what the spirit world is like from both sides of the veil. From current beliefs, communication, and energy exchange to being a death doula, Salicrow writes with firsthand knowledge, and it shows. This book will not disappoint!"

CAT GINA COLE, AUTHOR OF
PSYCHIC SKILLS FOR MAGIC AND WITCHCRAFT

"*Spirit Speaker* offers invaluable psychic insight combined with the author's deep tradition, family ideals, and ancestral knowledge designed to teach us how to keep the connection with our loved ones from beyond the veil. This book presents the death process as hope and understanding, encouraging us to create a sacred practice in which we make time and hold space for our loved ones in spirit. It beautifully and honorably expands the mind as well as the heart and assists the reader to embrace the idea that death touches us all."

SUZANNE WORTHLEY, AUTHOR OF
AN ENERGY HEALER'S BOOK OF DYING

"Written from a deep well of experience, respect, empathy, and love for those who are making, or have made, the transition to the spirit world and their beloved families. Throughout this manual of how to care compassionately for the dead and dying, Salicrow weaves personal stories with a lightness that is medicine for a culture that has been taught to fear death."

SIERRA MCFEETERS, FOUNDER OF
THE INDIGENOUS ROOTS INSTITUTE

"As a death doula educator and home funeral guide, I know that my students are always looking for ways to connect to their own beloved dead and also to help others. *Spirit Speaker* is invaluable for those seeking deeper connection to the spirit world and to implement ceremony and meaning into their lives. And personally, as a developing Medium, I have found the stories and tips a great resource."

ANNE-MARIE KEPPEL, AUTHOR OF *DEATH NESTING:
THE HEART-CENTERED PRACTICES OF A DEATH DOULA*
AND FOUNDER OF VILLAGE DEATHCARE

"Salicrow has written a guide that normalizes the sacredness of death and dying and its connection to the living. Embedded in this book are techniques that explain the importance of daily ancestral work, healing bloodlines, and assisting people during and after passing, including how to work with tragic deaths. This book shows that in order to heal, one must know death, while embracing life."

SONYA-PRAJNA PATRICK, PH.D., DEATH-TENDING DOULA,
MAGICK/CONJURE WORKER, AND BONE READER

"Salicrow brings knowledge and wisdom to the unimaginable. Through *Spirit Speaker,* she offers peace to family members and individuals who struggle with grief, shame, guilt, and hopelessness associated with the death of a loved one by natural causes, addiction, suicide, or a traumatic death. Salicrow presents specific and feasible methods that anyone can follow to honor and connect with their loved ones. This book illuminates a path to reclaiming our connection to our deceased loved ones, ancestors, and ourselves. A truly inspiring portrayal of what lies beyond the veil."

TERRI MAYER THOMSEN, MAC, LADC,
ADDICTION SPECIALIST IN PRIVATE CLINICAL PRACTICE,
REIKI MASTER TEACHER, AND DRUID PRIESTESS

"I will pass along this wise and earthy book to many friends and family—as a genuinely helpful guide to engaging with those on the other side and as an invaluable and urgent reminder that the dead are ready and willing to show us how to live."

PERDITA FINN, COAUTHOR OF *THE WAY OF THE ROSE*
AND AUTHOR OF *TAKE BACK THE MAGIC*

"Salicrow actively brings the reader on a journey through death and dying, while providing tools to accustom and initiate end-of-life rites of passage within one's family and community."

DAMIEN A. ARCHAMBEAU, LMT, BCTMB,
REIKI AND YOGA INSTRUCTOR AND MYSTIC

SPIRIT SPEAKER

A MEDIUM'S GUIDE TO DEATH AND DYING

A Sacred Planet Book

Salicrow

Destiny Books

Rochester, Vermont

Destiny Books
One Park Street
Rochester, Vermont 05767
www.DestinyBooks.com

Text stock is SFI certified

Destiny Books is a division of Inner Traditions International

Sacred Planet Books are curated by Richard Grossinger, Inner Traditions editorial board member and cofounder and former publisher of North Atlantic Books. The Sacred Planet collection, published under the umbrella of the Inner Traditions family of imprints, includes works on the themes of consciousness, cosmology, alternative medicine, dreams, climate, permaculture, alchemy, shamanic studies, oracles, astrology, crystals, hyperobjects, locutions, and subtle bodies.

Cataloging-in-Publication Data for this title is available from the Library of Congress

ISBN 978-1-64411-728-6 (print)
ISBN 978-1-64411-729-3 (ebook)

Printed and bound in the United States by Lake Book Manufacturing, LLC
The text stock is SFI certified. The Sustainable Forestry Initiative® program promotes sustainable forest management.

10 9 8 7 6 5 4 3 2 1

Text design and layout by Virginia Scott Bowman
This book was typeset in Garamond Premier Pro and Gill Sans with Bruphy and Archerus Grotesque used as display typefaces

To send correspondence to the author of this book, mail a first-class letter to the author c/o Inner Traditions • Bear & Company, One Park Street, Rochester, VT 05767, and we will forward the communication, or contact the author directly at **www.salicrow.com**.

This book is dedicated to my Ancestor
William Thomas, whose Irish Traveler blood sings
within me, and to all who mourn their Beloved Dead.
May it help you find peace.

CONTENTS

FOREWORD

Sandycrow

THE LAST OF THE WINTER'S SNOW had fallen when my dad found his way home to his people to die. His body had been telling him for some time that death was near. His ancestors said the time had come for him to prepare his soul for the journey to the Summerland. As snow melted and day and night were in perfect balance, our work began. Using drum, rattle, and song, we shook the cobwebs free, clearing the doorway to his soul. Once inside we traveled down long forgotten paths and chaotic causeways, calling on our ancestors, guides, and the Great Spirit to lead the way. The road was treacherous, at times filled with monsters of pain, regret, and loss. Calling forth the warrior within, he journeyed through the darkness and into the summer's sun filled with joy and love.

It was a time of celebration, hellos and good-byes, hugs and laughter, and campfires and grandchildren. As the sun set earlier in the western sky and crickets sang, we began our work of helping him to release and leave the body. In a comfy chair with candle lit, he followed my drum out and over mountaintops and streams. By rattle and drum, he traveled into yesteryear and all tomorrows. Who he was, had been, and would always be, becoming one. By the time the last leaf fell, all monsters were slain and his spirit was clean. Altars set and fires aglow, we called in the ancestors. From here the ancestors would be his guide to the Summerland and beyond. My rattle would serve as tether to the land of the living.

On the cold winter's wind, the ancestors came. My father's journey to the Summerland began. Family gathered to say farewell and offer blessings on his journey. We sang songs of comfort and love as his spirit left the body. And just like that his new life as an ancestor began.

My father's passing was beautiful and bright. Although I would miss his big bear hugs, I was not left broken by his passing. I knew the work we did had linked us for eternity, and he was truly free to be his best self. With no regret, nothing left unsaid, and no monsters left unconquered, he entered the Summerland whole. He entered the cosmos as pure love. I count myself lucky every day to have been able to have this experience with my father. I thank my great-grandmother and ancestors for showing me the way to not fear death but to embrace it. They showed me that our spirit never dies and that our relations with the dead are alive and ever evolving.

I cried when I read this powerful work by my sister. I did not cry from sorrow but from joy. In these pages there is hope and healing, not just for those left behind but for those who are crossing or have crossed already to the Summerland of the setting sun. From ancestor altars to communicating with our Beloved Dead, this book serves as a manual to understand the world of the dead. It also shows us how to become Wisdom Keepers and heal our ancestral lines.

Although this book is short in page, its work is profound and will remove the fear of what we all must face someday. It is a succinct and unique field guide that addresses the greatest mystery of all: death. Where do we go? How can we connect with our beloved on both sides of the veil? How do we heal and gain strength and serenity?

My sister Salicrow has done the remarkable and has made simple what has always seemed a confusing and complicated process. I am so proud of what she has accomplished, which is truly an act of love. I plan on giving each of my clients a copy of this book to help ease their pain and send them on the path to healing.

Peace and love,
Sandycrow

Sandycrow lives in a little big house on the edge of the woods in the rolling green hills of Vermont. There she supports her community, acting as not only death doula to those transitioning to the great beyond but also as clergy comforting those left behind and working with them to create a funeral that honors their Beloved Dead.

"Enchantress" by Robin Lee Wedemeyer

Gift from the Departed
EMILY GREY SHURR

opening into
All That Is
there is a certain relief
when we reach
past the density
of this incarnate world
into the Beyond, Void, Eternity
and
there is a tenderness
we feel
for the flesh, the body,
the material of it all
:
where Home is
flips
over the course of a lifetime
"Out there" . . .
"In here" . . .
"Here and Now" . . .
"With You" . . .
"By Myself" . . .

✦

there's something about
the Rhythm
of In & Out
Ebb & Flow
Home & Away
it's the contrast
that makes us know
we're alive
& everything changes
so it is
with Life & Death
that portal where
the pulse takes place
Creation—Destruction—
Creation—Destruction—
Light & Dark
Freedom & Bondage

✦

male & female
is one outward and one inward?
does it seem so?
which is which?
in the visible realm, the obvious,

masculine is outward &
feminine is inward
in the no less real world we do not see
(or do we?)
males are contained to an extreme,
beaten straight like swords, built impenetrable
like towers
and
females are generous and pulsing
pouring fragrance and invitation like flowers
(is this too a myth?)

✱

so here's the Beauty of the binary
the 1s and 0s
the either-ors
it's the Spanda
of differentiation
the moment
of separation
the churning
both either and or
that makes this dimension
so appealing
to the formless

that's the kink:
density
(and levity)
ask any yogi
there's no
in-breath
without
its accompanying
out-breath
it's absurd to even
try to imagine
the one
without
the other
they exist
only and ever
in an unending chain
a sequence
with no beginning
without
the vertical
and the horizontal
there is no z-axis
without
the tension between "opposites"

the magnetism
and the repulsion
there's no momentum

✴

this, finally,
the Gift
from the Departed—
this reverence for incarnate life:
as we begin to comprehend
our Deaths
we begin to apprehend
our Lives

························· ✳ ·························

1

ANCESTORS AND GUIDES

---
*

Gathering to Go
Laura Gail Grohe

For a long time I was distracted by the daffodils.
With a dramatic flourish you would drop to the ground,
tenderly kiss the yellow face, and sing
"You are my sunshine, my only sunshine."
It was only when I saw your hands shaking from fatigue and pain
that I realized why ground flowers called to you to lie with them.

For a long time I was distracted by your embrace of simplicity.
You had always been generous with your love and time,
why not your possessions as well?
A family painting to a beloved cousin in college to ease her
    loneliness,
your second favorite chair to me so your arms could hold me
    anytime I wanted.
It was only when I saw you had kept just
one cup, one bowl, a spoon, a knife, and a comfy bed
that I realized why you had given away your earthly goods.

For a long time I was distracted by your new ability to listen
　　silently
as family and friends chattered like birds.
It was only after I got the flu that I realized how exhausting it is
　　to talk,
and why your words were parceled out like precious nuggets.

It was only when I sat with you
under the ugly lights in that pristine white room,
and held your hand as your chest fell for the last time
that I realized how long you had been saying good-bye.

Death touches all of us; moving, shaking, and rearranging that which we call normal. When we lose someone we love we are often thrown into a whirlwind of emotions as we struggle to make sense of our life without them. Amplifying this feeling of loss is the separation modern culture has created around death and dying; something that is particularly true of first world nations. I believe this disconnect, particularly in the United States, was created in part by television's portrayal of what it means to be American as presented to the masses in the 1950s and 1960s. Suddenly all the cultural traditions of our multiethnic country were whitewashed into a *Leave It to Beaver* vanilla smoothy that left little room for venerating the dead. Life was about living, and no one wanted to be bothered with the unpleasantness of death and dying!

This hollow view of death has failed us. We need more; we desire knowledge and an understanding of the death process. We can no longer look away. It feels wrong for our loved one's last moments to be handled by the sterile hands of hospitals and funeral homes. It's not that these places should be shunned, just that they are not enough! This separation from the fate we all eventually embrace has left us soul sick. While some find solace in the perspectives presented by religion, most find that these still lack depth and come with few substantial answers.

Having grown up in a family with psychic gifts, I learned that it was a privilege to have contact with the spirit world and that with this advantage came responsibility to both the living and the dead. I knew at a young age that everyone has the ability to experience our Beloved Dead—the ancestors, guides, and loved ones connected to us—and that like all things, some people are better at it than others. I was fortunate that my family kept our traditions around death. My great-grandmother Grammy Brown was the matriarch of the family and the most important person in my young life. Grammy was half Irish Traveler (an Irish nomadic indigenous ethnic group) and half Blackfoot (an indigenous people of North America). Both of her parents were psychically gifted and shared their cultural traditions with her, which she in turn shared with me. These teachings were not only on how to communicate with the dead but also on how to give honor and respect to our ancestors, who paved the path before us. With these teachings in mind, I have made it my practice to share what I know of the spirit world with my clients, including ceremonies and practices that help create a living connection with our Beloved Dead.

ANCESTOR ALTARS

To venerate is to give honor or show respect for something. Venerating the dead is the act of creating a sacred practice in which we make time and hold space for our loved ones in spirit. It is an act of love, and it carries great healing potential, giving us a healthy way to express the sorrow and grief we feel at our loved one's passing. After all, the hardest part of someone's death is dealing with their absence!

One of the easiest ways to start a relationship with our Beloved Dead is by creating an ancestor altar. An altar is a shelf, table, or cabinet set aside for spiritual or religious purposes. Items placed on an altar are done so with intention, chosen for their energetic significance or sentimental value. Ancestor altars are specifically focused on loved ones who have crossed into spirit and can be created as individual shrines or family altars. Altars erected for individuals are often created with healing in mind, giving those who mourn a place to grieve, whereas altars connected to our family/tribe are more traditionally places utilized to honor our ancestors and ask them for guidance. Both are places of magic and healing.

Ancestor altars are not meant to be stagnant. Instead, they are meant to change and grow as our relationship with our Beloved Dead evolves. It is my hope that through this book you gain a deeper understanding of the afterlife and rekindle a relationship with your Beloved Dead. Know that it all begins with a simple act of remembrance such as this.

Many of us already have the makings of such shrines scattered throughout our homes, and some of us have whole rooms dedicated to our dead—mausoleums that keep us locked in our pain while simultaneously giving us comfort. These tombs to our dead may feel necessary, as we desperately try to hold on to whatever remains we can. While it may seem appealing on some level to keep things as they were, locking their belongings away as if in a time capsule, we trap part of ourselves in the moment of our deepest sorrow. Altars consolidate the bits we have strewn about, giving us a localized place to focus our mourning in a healthy way, which helps us begin the process of moving on. Altars, unlike time-capsule bedrooms, are meant to evolve over time like living things. Where the bedroom mausoleum imprisons both the living and the dead in a place of unwavering sorrow, a constant reminder of that which we lost, the altar presents a place to heal and create a relationship with our loved one in spirit.

In acute mourning it is often necessary to leave things exactly as they were, thereby giving those who mourn a bit of time to adjust to such a sudden and painful change. However, to heal we must move on with life, we must heal, for we do our dead no justice when we metaphorically die along with them! Please note when I mention moving on that I am not suggesting that we put our loved one behind us or forget the pain; I am simply saying that at some point the bereaved must return to the world of the living. We must find moments of joy, love, and tenderness again, for our loved ones in spirit are watching us, and when we stay locked in our grief, so do they!

Altars created for the recently departed, as well as the dead we will never fully get over, are much like three-dimensional scrapbooks representing who our loved ones were in life. They are created with pictures showing how we remember them best, personal items the once owned, and things that remind us of them. When choosing a place for a personal shrine I recommend creating it in a room the beloved preferred to spend time in, as their spirit will be naturally drawn to such places. The dead often speak of their favorite places during spirit communication sessions, sharing how they spent most of their time in the kitchen smoking cigarettes, or how they loved watching birds through the sliding glass door in the living room.

These familiar and beloved places are the best locations for altars dedicated to individuals.

Family altars are best placed in the living room or kitchen depending on the type of family you are. If your family gathers in the kitchen around large meals and a hot stove, then that is where your ancestor altar belongs. If instead your memories revolve around watching the game or movies in the living room, all comfy on the couch, then your family shrine belongs there. When creating a sacred space for our ancestors, we want to see it as a place of joy and becoming, for all of the people we honor are also our guides, our cheerleaders, and our teachers. They inspire us and comfort us, and the path they walked before us helped forge who we are today.

Sometimes people feel the need for both forms of altars in their homes. This can be accomplished by having more than one altar or by combining the two, with the center of the shrine focused on the individual you actively mourn and the memorabilia connected to the rest of your ancestors surrounding them as a form of support. In this way you are not only mourning your recently dead, you are also asking for the spirits of your family to welcome them home and guide them in their transition.

Once your altar is created it is helpful to spend time with it each day, lighting a candle and sitting for a few minutes in prayer or talking to your Beloved Dead. Come as you are, be real, and remember who they were and the relationship you had with them in life. Drink your coffee with them, share stories of the family, ask them for support, and allow yourself to be fully present. This means making the conscious effort to leave behind your everyday worries for just a few moments. We need to sit at our altar in much the same way that we enter a cemetery, with our mind sincerely centered on how much we miss our loved ones. The more regularly we use our altar, the easier it will become to perceive when our loved ones are with us, because sacred shrines become stronger and stronger connecters to the spirit world the more actively we engage with them.

OFFERINGS

Another way to interact with our Beloved Dead is through the act of giving offerings. The best offerings come in the form of the simple things they loved. Their favorite foods or drinks are wise choices, as are cigarettes, marijuana, and alcohol. In fact, the things most spirits love to talk about are food, drink, and smoke. We love those ingestible bits when we're alive and miss them when we die. While a spirit cannot actually eat a piece of pumpkin pie, they can enjoy the memory of it! They love it when we eat, drink, and smoke their favorite things or leave such things as offerings on the family altar. My dad and great-grandmother were both smokers, which means I often place cigarettes on my altar, and on occasion I smoke a cigarette for them. Of course, these things will not disappear if you leave them on your altar, as spirits are not actually consuming the items—they are enjoying the energy of them, so remember to clean up your altar before things spoil. Items removed from an altar may be disposed of in the same manner you would dispose of regular food or drink.

Not all offerings have to be consumable. Songs and stories, particularly those that tell of our ancestor's deeds, are also great offerings, as are religious items, bits of jewelry, wooden spoons, and recipe cards. Playing your grandfather's favorite music while you tell your children tales of his misadventures and dancing around the room in fancy dress as you think of your favorite aunt are also beautiful ways to give honor to our Beloved Dead. Other offerings may come in the form of flowers, driftwood from their favorite ocean spot, or items we find that make us think of them.

SIGNS AND SYMBOLS

The spirits of our Beloved Dead are constantly connecting with us and often try to communicate with us through signs and symbols. The effort that they will go to for our attention is remarkable and endless in its possibilities. While most spirits try techniques that have been used by others and recognizable by the living masses, some reach for the obscure, and some truly impress me with the persistency of their communications.

Whether it be alphabets or mystical icons, our thoughts are activated by symbolism. Religion and spirituality utilize this truth often, bestowing power on or through holy symbols. This innate understanding of the symbolic language is something spirits rely upon in their communication. Often when I connect families to their Beloved Dead, I will be shown symbols that connect to memories between the spirit and their living loved ones.

A grandfather showing me a purple colored heart will often bring the family to tears as the image gives them reassurance that this spirit truly is the one they seek, knowing he had received a Purple Heart medal for his military service. The spirit of a child smiling at me and showing me a rainbow over and over again makes sense to the mourning parents who have a picture of their daughter, with a rainbow painted on her cheek, still hanging on her bedroom wall. In addition to spirits using symbols to communicate through mediums, they also use them to connect directly with their living loved ones. In fact, it is one of the most common things they do, showing us dimes, feathers, butterflies, and Elvis.

While most spirits use symbols with personal significance to make contact with the living, they also use symbols and signs that are more universal in nature, such as cardinals, crows, and jays. There is a powerful connection between these songbirds and the spirit world, in part due to their strong relationship with humans, as these birds are bolder in nature and interested in the human habitat. While other birds are used, too, they are less common and usually hold some kind of personal connection. Interestingly, spirits will use images of the birds as seen on greeting cards or art as often as they use the birds themselves, directing their energy at the image in the hope that their living loved one will sense them and recognize the symbolic connection between such birds and the dead.

Another favorite sign given by spirits comes in the form of songs played on the radio. Many of us can relate to the experience of riding in our car and having a song come on that nearly brings us to tears, as we immediately feel the presence of our Beloved Dead with us. This marvel, while often unexplained, appears to be one of the most emotionally moving and hard-to-disbelieve experiences people can have. I believe this is due to the vibration of the music combined with the spirit contact, which moves us in a profoundly emotional way. It is important to understand in the case of songs on the radio that the DJ is completely left out of the loop; they have no part in the communication. If our Beloved Dead are visiting us when a song that they have a connection with comes on, they push their energy at us in the hope that we will feel them through the music. The emotional effect of the song opens our aura, making us more sensitive to their energy. When a spirit sees that they have made a successful contact this way, they will repeat the action over and over again in the hope of creating a bonded connection that allows us to recognize them when they are around.

While this is remarkable, I have experienced far more astonishing and persistent phenomenon connected to music and spirits. In the case of persistency, my Aunt Sheila takes the cake. Being a pushy and determined soul from a family known for its spiritual gifts, she was immediately adept at getting my attention. At her funeral ceremony she began repeating the chorus from Rupert Holmes's song "Escape (The Pina Colada Song)," which I personally can't stand! I finally asked her best friend if Sheila had a connection to the song, and sure enough it was one of her favorites. For years my aunt used the annoyance of this song to get my attention whenever she needed me to check in on her daughter or pass on a message for her. Over time I grew to hate the song more and more, not because of the association with my aunt, but because I didn't like it to begin with and would rather it not be an earworm stuck in my mind.

One day she reached out playing "Take It on the Run" by REO Speedwagon. I was stunned and stopped in my tracks, asking her what made her change her song. She replied that my father had told her she would get further with me if she didn't choose music that I found annoying. This experience shows how she evolved her use of song to communicate over time. It is also a reminder to you that your Beloved Dead may put the music into your mind as easily as they push their energy at you when the song comes on the radio.

Many of our Beloved Dead are drawn to communicating through radios and other electronic devices in more audibly noticeable ways. I have personally experienced, as have many of my clients, spirits manipulating the volume on phones, radios, televisions, and anything else that has adjustable sound, something that has only increased in frequency as our devices have moved into digital format. Along with volume dials, they love to trigger smoke alarms, lights, GPSs, and electronic toys. Once, during a personal spirit communication, I was relaying a message, saying, "John is telling me you need a guide, that you are running off into the horizon without a clue where you are going," at the same time the GPS on the woman's phone announced, "GPS signal lost, redirecting." That was not a coincidence!

Coins are another form of communication utilized by spirits. Dimes and pennies are the most common, but some spirits use signature coins such as fifty-cent pieces or two-dollar coins. In the case of common pennies and dimes, the spirit is relying on the fact that such things are small and often displaced. They are not making coins appear from the ether; there are no pennies falling from heaven. Instead, they are again throwing their energy at us. Having spotted the coin first themselves, they take advantage of our symbolic language, hoping that we will remember the connection between coins and spirit contact. Energetically they are directing themselves into the coin, illuminating it with their essence.

The use of symbols in spirit communication can be used by spirits in multiple ways, with spirits generally choosing a few symbols that hold personal connection between them and their living loved ones. Whether it be a shamrock, the United States flag, a peace sign, or a flamingo, they will direct their energy at their chosen symbol over and over again in the hope of catching our eye and getting us to see the signs! Along with experiencing these images in our waking world, we may also experience symbolic communication with our Beloved Dead in our dreams, as it is a favorite place for spirits to reach out in communication.

Dreams are one of the easiest places to receive communication from the dead, as we do not censor our dreams; instead, we place our rational thinking mind in the passenger seat and allow our intuitive subconscious to guide the show. We are open and believe anything is possible in our dreams! This belief works in our Beloved Dead's favor, as they no longer have to batter their way through the rational shield of our analytical mind. For those seeking contact with their personal spirits, I highly recommend keeping track of your dreams as well as experiences during guided meditation or journeywork. It is helpful to get a dream interpretation book, as spirits will utilize common symbols and images, as well as those that have a personal resonance. Although in the latter case, you will not need definitions from a book, as those symbols will trigger you personally.

Many spirits are just winging it, and regardless of our desire to have them show us one specific symbol that would prove they are with us, they may not be able to. In truth, they may not remember it as vividly as we do, or they simply may not be skilled enough in communication to get that message through. We need to meet them halfway, understanding that they may be communicating with us in the only way they know how. Not all spirits are equal in their communication ability! This is something any skilled medium understands, as some communication is smooth as silk and clear as a bell, filled with direct telepathy, symbolism, visuals, sightings, smells, and the whole shebang! Others communications are like playing a sophisticated game of charades with someone you have never met and who speaks a different language. To be a medium requires great skill in translation!

One of my favorite signs sent by Beloved Dead comes in the form of a smell. It is truly remarkable to me how clearly and easily spirits can trigger our olfactory senses. While I believe most of these experiences are happening within our consciousness, I have experienced groups in which everyone expressed smelling the same scent. One experience in particular stands out. I was teaching a spirit communication class focused on psychometry. (Psychometry is the psychic art of retrieving information from the spirit world and the unknown through holding an inanimate item.) Everyone was instructed to bring an item, and each item was passed around to the members of the group, who then shared any thoughts they had picked up from the object. One of the women had brought a small enamel cup that had been used by her grandfather for many years to test the maple sap being boiled in the family sugarhouse. She did not tell anyone anything about the cup, yet every person in the class claimed to smell maple syrup as the cup was being passed around. It was such a visceral experience that they were declaring it out loud, not waiting for their turn to hold the cup. (It should be noted that the woman whose cup it was came from an old Vermont family with some spiritual gifts running in their veins.)

I could most likely write an entire book on the ways spirits reach out for connection, but this is not that book. This is a book of hope and understanding, meant to be a guide to the otherworld (world of spirit), with my hope being that anyone reading it may find a deeper understanding about what happens when we die and of how "alive" our Beloved Dead really are. When we open our consciousness and begin to understand that we do not cease to exist when we leave our body in death, then we begin to live our life with a deeper sense of purpose and joy. When we become open to the many ways our dead are utilizing to communicate with us, we feel less lonesome, as we realize we are never really alone. This is something I not only understand but also utilize as a medium. Knowing that my spirits are always with me, I never walk into a dark parking lot without first having my spiritual doorman, Adam, or my father scout the perimeter. While you may not be able to work with your spirits with such clarity, you can call on Grandma to stand beside you when you're going through hard times, and you can lean on your dad when you're scared and lonesome.

One of the things I recommend to all of my students is keeping a sacred journal, or Book of Shadows. A Book of Shadows is not meant to be a diary filled with our emotional processes or everyday life events. Instead it is meant to be a recording of our deepest spiritual workings. In working through our understanding of death and dying, regardless of whether it is an act of personal healing or self-development, it is beneficial to keep track of the signs and symbols we experience, understanding that spirit communication is not something done by our Beloved Dead but instead a connection created between us and our Beloved Dead. Just as we are reliant on their cleverness and ingenuity, they must rely on our channeling ability and the flexibility of our mind to receive messages. Like any skill, it takes practice and tracking.

I invite you to move through this book as a seeker of both healing and awareness. We are living in changing times in which the human race is going through a global climate crisis and a psychic evolution. Our awareness is expanding as a species. We have reached the tipping point where it is no longer just those on a path of psychic knowledge who are experiencing supernatural phenomenon; it is also happening to those of us who were content in our physical realities of jobs, vacations at the beach, and shopping for something special. Within this time of evolving consciousness, the veil between the worlds of the living and the dead is dissolving, becoming a gossamer thing that separates us more by suggestion than the force of a true barrier. We must open our mind to the possibility and release doubt, for when we do, we will see how miraculous the world really is!

SPIRIT GUIDES

My dad was a good one for asking practical questions about the spirit world, sometimes calling me just to ask simple things, such as "Do spirits sit in chairs, kid?" or "Do spirits have jobs?" The answer to the first question is dependent on the spirit. While spirits do not get tired and therefore have no need to sit, they may enjoy the act of doing so. Some spirits go to great lengths to continue patterns they created in the living world, going as far as to re-create "space" around themselves that is similar to their homes, offices, and beloved landscapes from life. Others put little energy at all into being anything, content to exist as observers of their past incarnations and the people and stories connected to them.

When we die, we become all that we ever were. Our soul slips into a state of wholeness in which we are able to interact with the multi-lifetime version of our being. While this image may not fit into the religious teachings presented to many of us in childhood, it does not go against it either, for religion simply uses different words to express this feeling of completion.

People who arrive at death with unprocessed trauma often need more time to review the life they just exited, as there is much to process there. While it may seem grossly unfair that we are not able to avoid our life story in death, we do so from a different perspective, with both our emotions and viewpoints adjusted. This is something I talk about in more detail later in the book. While what these souls experience is more limited in its possibilities, they are given a sheltered environment in which deep healing can take place.

For an emotionally healthy person, death is like slipping on your favorite sweater, warm and comforting, with a feeling of contentment. Spirits who have entered death in a good, centered space often find themselves in the role of spirit guides. While they do not spend every waking moment watching over us, having little concern for whether we floss our teeth or do the dishes, they are with us when we need them. When we are endangered or emotionally upset, it is as if an alarm goes off alerting them to our distress. In my mind I imagine it like an insect landing on a spider's web: our need creates a vibration on the web, sending out a signal that we are in need of support.

In my experience what people refer to as their guardian angel is in fact an ancestral spirit guide. While I do believe in angels, I believe they are high-vibration beings who only interact with humans when the need arises, and they are generally not hanging out watching Bob on his morning commute to the mini mart. They are a bigger force in the spirit world, and interactions with them are generally remarkable and life altering.

All of us come into life with a guide on board in the spirit world. Many of these guides are relatives who died close to the time of our birth or family and friends close to our parents or to us when we were babies. The guide joined to us in many ways helps keep us on track with the items we placed on our life agenda before birth.*

Ancestral spirit guides are the spirits connected to us through blood or other lifetimes. They are often connected to more than one person in the same family/soul group and work with us on bigger spiritual endeavors, such as healing family wounds or breaking ancestral curses (destructive patterns and behaviors, such as addiction and abuse). Such guides are older souls with more wisdom. While they are not walking with us through every job interview

---

*It is my belief that before coming into each incarnation we create an outline that contains the lessons we have chosen to experience at planned times in our life. These happenings show up to psychic readers as karmic events in the person's life.

and emotionally charged moment of our life, they are with us in our darkest hours and our greatest moments of growth, particularly when such things are in alignment with the healing of family wounds. These guides often hold another important role in the family: the role of matriarch/patriarch, the family ancestor who gathers the dead, attending to the greeting of all family members as they cross into spirit. While a spirit may often comment on being greeted by their husband, wife, or child, it is common that along with one's life partner they are met by a mother, grandmother, or father who was known to be the glue that held the family together in their lifetime.

People who are working on expanding their spiritual consciousness will often find themselves with other guides in addition to the ones connected to their family. These others are generally connected to us through past/parallel lives and come in to our lives when we are ready to open our minds to a broader view of reality. This is happening for many as we move from 3-D reality into 5-D reality, coming online to an awareness of all that we are and all we have been. Through contact with these teaching guides, we learn much about our other incarnations and through them often find healing for wounds and fears we could never explain. Understanding that we are souls experiencing physical reality through the lens of multiple lifetimes is the goal of contact with such guides.

There are some who go through their lives without ever having an awareness of the guides watching over them, but the belief in spirit guides is one of the most acceptable forms of spirit connection there is. Regardless of religious doctrine, many of us attest to sensing or knowing that we have some form of spiritual guardian watching over us. Mediums are often aware of the presence of a person's spirit guide shortly after a child is born and separated from the mother's body. In some cases, this guide can be detected while the child is still in utero. This is more likely to happen if the spirit coming in has a significant purpose to attain in life or is spiritually gifted. Such was my case as, while my mother was pregnant with me, Grammy Brown communicated with Peter, one of my guides, who told her that I would be a medium. With this knowledge she began preparing me for my role as a medium while I was a preschooler.

We all have a spirit guide, each and every one of us, and some of us have multiple guides. It is not uncommon to have a guide step into our consciousness to work with us through particular life events, lending their strength and expertise as support. One of the easiest ways to make contact with our guides is through a professional medium. Doing so can provide clear instruction on what your guide has been trying to communicate to you, as well as offering the opportunity to get clear on the best ways to develop personal communication with our guides.

Whether you are exploring work with your guides on your own or through a professional, remember to record your experiences. If you are working with a medium, make sure to ask them if you can record your session, as going back over the recording provides an opportunity to glean more information from the experience. Remember to record your experiences in your Book of Shadows/ sacred journal and start speaking to your guide as if they can hear you clearly, because they can. Your guides can hear you whether you speak out loud or in your head. That said, I recommend speaking out loud if you are able as it keeps the mind from wandering and makes us more aware of the fact that we are actively interacting with spirit.

2

TIME, SPACE, AND PERCEPTION

MEDIUMS ARE PEOPLE WHO HAVE a more open connection to the world of spirit than most people, allowing them to channel communication from beyond the veil of death. Naturally more open to the otherworld, they have a heightened psychic sensitivity that allows them to perceive spirits. Like all things, innate ability does not guarantee skill, which is something that must be developed through practice and technique. Many who are born open to the other side never become proficient in communicating due to the fear and dogma they have been exposed to throughout their life, and in many cases the experience is traumatic for them because they do not understand what is truly happening.

THE VEIL BETWEEN THE WORLDS

The barrier between the worlds of the living and the dead is often referred to as a veil because it is perceived as gossamer in nature, an illusional separation more than a solid barrier. Crossing it requires a suspension of disbelief, a releasing of the programming that claims we are disconnected from our loved ones in spirit. Like looking through a veil, our vision of the otherworld is cloudy, with thoughts and images often leaving our perception as quickly as they enter it. Our experience of the spirit world is often fleeting, for the dead lack physical form, and projecting an image of themselves takes energy. They must borrow this energy from outside sources, such as natural mediums and the Earth's energetic ley lines.

When it comes to communication, spirits require a power supply outside of themselves to manipulate the physical world. Things such as audible sounds, phantom smells, and apparitions* take a lot of energy to manifest.

Mediums are natural conduits, meaning they provide an easy power supply for the spirit world. Because of this, many spirit speakers drain batteries, meaning that phones, watches, and other electrical devices worn on or near their body often loose power rapidly. I have personally been aware of this phenomenon in my own life since I was about seven or eight years old, and the first gift my husband ever gave me was a wind-up watch; a way of telling me he was paying attention to the things I said and remembered I drained batteries.

When a medium is actively communicating, the spirit they are speaking to is borrowing their energy. I like to imagine it like the magic pool/mana in a video game, which recharges when a player stops using their magic, the spirit speaker's energy returns quickly when the communication ends. People who have natural ability but lack education and skill may find they are often exhausted, not realizing that their energy is constantly being tapped by the dead. Learning how to protect one's personal energy and allowing it to be used only when we choose is important for those who are sensitive to spirit.

---

*An apparition is a ghost, phantom, or illusional image.

A simple technique for protecting one's energy if you feel you are being tapped by spirit is to get in the practice of scanning your energetic body. You can do this by simply sitting or lying still and focusing your attention on your body. Take a few deep breaths to center yourself and, starting at your feet, begin moving your consciousness up your body, looking for anything that doesn't feel like you. When you connect with an energy that feels foreign or outside your personal energy field, allow yourself to trace it back, imagining you are following a metallic cord. If the image of a living person comes to mind, you will not be surprised to see that it is someone with whom you have unresolved issues, or someone you care greatly about who is in dire straits. If instead you find that it becomes slippery or illusional, its appearance mutable, it is most likely a spirit. *This does not necessarily mean you are being psychically attacked!* Spirits are often doing this innocently, more like a cat drawn to a sun spot rather than an entity maliciously out to devour us. In truth, encounters with "evil spirits" are rare, and more often than not the recipient has been the victim of abuse or trauma in their physical world or comes from a religiously restrictive background that contained dogma filled with demons and devils.

Once you have determined where you are being tapped, simply disengage from the connection. You can do this by imagining you are removing the cord from your energetic body* or saying out loud with authority, "I do not give you permission to use my energy. It is not okay for you to do so!" As this energy is truly ours, the decision to take it back is often enough to stop the tapping. However, if you are experiencing energetic draining from spirit and are unable to protect yourself from it after trying these simple techniques, I

---

*This is not like cord removal in shamanism. It is far easier, as the connection is most often innocent and lacking an emotional component.

recommend reaching out to a professional medium for help.

People who are natural mediums are more likely to have spirit activity happen around them, and I learned at a young age the importance of regulating and guarding my energy. Mediums not only experience the dead themselves, they also make it possible for others to do so. If you were living in a house that was known to be haunted, but no one in your family had any ability as a spirit channel, then more often than not nothing would happen. Without the power supply provided by the medium, the spirits lack the energy needed to manipulate the physical world.

The exception to the rule is if there are strong ley lines running under or around the home. Ley lines are the underground water and magnetic lines of our planet. Like the blood vessels and meridians of the human body, these lines carry the vital energy of the planet from place to place. People living and working in homes and offices that have powerful energy lines running under or through them are often more likely to experience spirit activity. When there is either a natural medium living in a home or a strong ley line nearby, spirits are more active, as they have ample energy to fuel their antics, and even those who are psychically limited can experience spirit phenomenon.

As more of us are energetically activated by the psychic evolution taking place within our species, we are becoming more aware of the unseen world as the veil between the living and the dead becomes sheerer and sheerer.* We are coming into a time in which

---

*Traditionally the veil has been known to be thin during the time around Beltane (May 1) and Samhain/Halloween (October 31) and thicken back up again as the wheel of the year moves into the summer and winter solstices. However, it has been noted by the psychically sensitive that in the past few years the veil has not returned to its thicker state, that instead it is thinning at Beltane and then thinning again at Samhain. Because it is not returning to its denser state, more and more people are beginning to have personal experiences with the spirit world.

our ancestors walk among us, and the grief of death can be eased with the knowledge that our Beloved Dead are not truly gone but have simply returned to spirit form.

BETWIXT AND BETWEEN

We have been trained to believe that our existence is based on solid form, when, in fact, this is just part of our reality. As a child I would lie in bed questioning which of my experiences were the true reality: those that I lived in the physical world or those I had while dreaming and mirror gazing. In the end I came to the conclusion that both were real for me and began intentionally walking the border between worlds.

"Betwixt and between" refers to moments in time that are neither here nor there, day nor night, spring nor summer, fall nor winter. Halloween, which lies directly between the autumnal equinox and the winter solstice is such a time, as are dawn and dusk. In such times, psychically sensitive people often experience heightened awareness and an enchanted or dreamlike atmosphere. Places on the Earth that are located on ley lines share this quality of slippery time and space. In such times and places, it is easier for our minds to enter a light-trance state, much like the state of consciousness we experience before falling asleep, and in the betwixt and between the veil separating the worlds is at its thinnest.

While everyone has the potential for contacting spirits, the skill necessary to do so at will must be developed, and it requires a significant amount of natural ability. This natural ability can reveal itself in random experiences with spirit throughout one's life, such as seeing one's grandparent standing at the end of their bed on the night the grandparent dies or hearing noises when staying in a house that's haunted. As I explained earlier, spirits require an energy source, and that energy comes from the Earth or a medium. But while a skilled medium is able to communicate with the dead whenever and wherever they like, those who are not naturally inclined to experience the dead and/or those who are seeking to develop skill would be wise to stack their deck by using every advantage, and that includes working within the betwixt and between.

Dawn and dusk are moments of the betwixt and between we can utilize every day. They are still moments when there is a heaviness on the land, and the sun below the horizon casts long shadows and turns the world to shades of gray. There is something sacred about these dreamy, in-between moments. Those of us who rise early enough to greet the dawn recognize the heightened awareness that accompanies it, as the slightest sound or movement seems bold and brash in the quietness of daybreak. Dusk can similarly alter awareness, and, like dawn, it is a time of distorted shadows and wibbly-wobbliness; however, it is more languid, noted by all the folks who need a dose of caffeine or a catnap as the sun is setting. The altered state of consciousness experienced at these times greatly enhances the connection to our Beloved Dead!

If you are seeking to connect with your Beloved Dead, choosing to do so at dawn or dusk will enhance the experience for you, as it allows your consciousness to be soft around the edges. Try sitting at your altar at one of these times. Make it a regular practice, a scheduled visiting time with your spirits. Allow your mind to wander and let go of the words *maybe, kinda,* and *could be.* Be persistent, and your sensitivity to their presence will grow.

A MEDIUM'S STATE OF MIND

While mediums may receive messages in a variety of forms and develop different methods for doing so, all mediums enter a state of trance* to receive them. Just as there are different psychic techniques for processing communication between the two sides of the veil, there are also different states of trance in which we can access our intuitive minds and process incoming messages. Most mediums work in a light- to medium-trance state, as entering a deep trance is not necessary for receiving communication from the spirit world.

A light trance feels like that sweet, drowsy state of consciousness we experience when listening to relaxing music or rock in a rocking chair. In this state our mind drifts easily but is still aware enough to be pulled back into ordinary consciousness by any cause for alarm. People often find themselves naturally in this state while daydreaming, and spirits often communicate with us in the dream state, so make note of the thoughts that cross your mind while in a dreamy condition.

A medium trance is a deeper state of consciousness in which our intuitive mind is running the show, and our analytical, thinking mind is put in the passenger seat. It is most often achieved intentionally, through hypnogogic techniques designed for exactly that purpose, such as journeywork, guided meditation, drumming, or hypnosis. In this state we are less aware of the external world and generally ignore background noise and nonalarming stimulus. You may have experienced this state when receiving Reiki or other

---

*A trance is a semiconscious state in which a person is only partially aware of external stimuli. While such states can come about involuntarily, they are most often induced intentionally through modalities such as hypnosis, journeywork, or guided meditation.

energetic healing work or when listening to a recording of Native American drumming. If you entered a medium-trance state, you most likely felt deeply relaxed, possibly experiencing vivid colors or visions in your mind, and "awoke" at the end of the session feeling as if you had dozed off. It can be tricky to develop this state of consciousness to a point at which you receive visions, but when you are able to, you can use techniques like journeywork to seek out personal connection to your ancestral spirits and guides in the astral realm.

A deep trance resembles sleeping and is a state in which our analytical thinking mind is set aside. A person in a deep state of trance is not aware of their external surroundings and will be unresponsive to all but dramatic stimuli such as loud noises and being shaken awake. When a medium works in deep trance, they require an assistant to ask them questions. In this state of consciousness, the answers come directly from the spirit speaking through the medium or from the medium's higher self. It is not uncommon for the medium to have no recollection of the questions asked or answers given. A deep-trance state is difficult to attain and is generally not a practical way of channeling spirit, especially when the lighter states can be so effective. However, Edgar Cayce, one of the most famous psychics of our time, was known as "the sleeping prophet," because he channeled his messages in this state.

I spend a great deal of my time in a light-trance state, entering it every time I do a psychic reading or speak to someone's Beloved Dead. I enter the state easily, most often by rocking my upper body slightly, undulating in a rhythmic pattern—a movement so minor that most people don't even notice I am doing it. I also spin my rings and hold my gaze in a wide angle above the heads of the living people with whom I am connecting, engaging my peripheral vision. It takes me but a few breaths to enter this state. Like having a frequent-flyer pass, I am able to skip over the whole convincing myself to relax bit and get right to it! In this state of consciousness, I am able to enter the betwixt and between, to be both in the physical world with my clients and in the spirit world with their Beloved Dead. As a multisensory medium, my experience in this state is much like monitoring multiple computer screens at once.

🌿Contacting Your Beloved Dead

For those of you who are truly seeking personal contact with your Beloved Dead, my recommendation is to first learn how to consciously enter a light-trance state. One of the simplest ways to do so is to pull out that old rocking chair, especially if it belonged to your grandma or some other relative you may want to visit. Place it in the room where you have your altar, if you can, and rock in it at dawn or dusk. Allow the motion to gently rock your consciousness into a relaxed, lucid state and pay attention to the visions and thoughts that cross your mind. Remember, this takes practice, and if you find yourself doubting whether something is truly a message, it helps to keep this in mind: you can think thousands of thoughts at any given minute. What made you think that particular thought at that particular moment? If we spent as much time coming up with reasons why something *could* be a message, instead of why it *couldn't* be, we would experience miraculous events all the time!

WIDE-ANGLE VISION

This book is designed as a guide to the afterlife, answering the most common questions I am asked as a medium about what happens after death. However, I know that many of you reading this book are seeking personal connection, with the hope that you will be united with your Beloved Dead. With that in mind, these teachings are meant to give you the tools and techniques to have that experience. It is important, however, that we not judge our success in receiving contact as a sign of their love for us or lack thereof, for just as we can all do art but are not necessarily "artists," we all have the potential to receive messages from our Beloved Dead, but not all of us will have the ability to become a skilled medium. I say this so you will remember that it is more likely a lack of skill than a lack of love that keeps the experience at bay!

Often when people speak about seeing a spirit it goes something like this: "I saw something out of the corner of my eye, but when I turned to look it was gone!" The spirit was most often spotted when the person was relaxed, sleepy, or daydreaming, and the act of seeing them snapped their consciousness into an alert, searching mode. Turning to look directly where they saw the apparition generally results in it disappearing from view because they looked through the spirit!

The spirits of the dead exist in a different dimension from the living. It is my understanding that these realities exist in the same space but resonate at a different vibration. I often describe these dimensions through the use of clear and translucent colored folders, the kind you use for book reports that come in clear, blue, green, pink, and yellow. In this analogy we exist in the reality represented by the clear folder, the world of the dead is represented by the blue folder, the elemental/natural world is represented by the green, and so on. While we can all perceive the physical world—represented by the clear folder—not everyone has the ability to see into the other colors, which I compare to being color-blind. While there will most certainly be varying levels of skill, we all are capable of expanding our vision through practice and techniques. It starts by learning how to look!

In the previous section we spoke about the different states of trance in which a medium works: light, medium, and deep. It is in the light trance that our consciousness is fluid and that we experience spiritual apparitions, as our mind is flexible enough to perceive the nonphysical realms. Seldom are spirits seen when we are actively engaged, as in those times our mind is way more focused on the activity. This is why photos of weddings and birthday parties can be loaded with orbs,* and the guests never noticed a thing.

In the beginning of my Druid training, I was introduced to the term *wide-angle vision* by my teacher Ivan McBeth. While the term was new, the technique was not, as I had used it most of my life, having been taught by my great-grandmother to "see" spirits by looking out of the corners of my eyes. In short, wide-angle vision is the act of switching the focus of our vision from forward-facing to peripheral. This simple act changes the way we perceive the world, allowing us a broader, yet less-detailed, view. While we may not take in as many details, we can get a bigger picture of the surroundings and, with practice, increase our likelihood of seeing our Beloved Dead, as it is through this veiled vision they are perceived.

The technique is really quite simple, and those of you who have ever hunted can simply employ the same vision you use when sitting in a deer stand. For those of you who have not hunted, I suggest engaging the process used for viewing the 3-D pictures that were popular in the 1990s and early 2000s, the ones that have a 3-D image "hidden" within an obvious 2-D image that can only be seen by letting your vision go wide. To do this place your focus on

---

*An orb is a transparent ball of light connected to spirits of the dead.

the space just past the tip of your nose. Your vision will blur a bit, don't worry, this is part of the process. Next, take a deep breath in and out through your nose, relaxing into the visual position. Keep taking deep breaths for a few moments, noticing what you see out of your peripheral vision through this method.

As a child I did something similar when looking at myself in the mirror. I would look down my nose and through the image in front of me until my vision blurred. I would practice and play with how I saw things whenever I stood in front of a mirror, expanding my vision to see what and who was around me. You may also want to try this yourself. After all, mirrors have long been powerful tools for seers and mediums and are often referred to as portals to the otherworld.

With time and practice wide-angle vision will become a natural way of viewing. Don't overthink it. Remember, hunters have been using this visionary style since the beginning of humanity. Practicing this technique will make it easier to use the next time you catch something out of the corner of your eye. The real key will be remembering to use it!

TIME IS WOBBLY

Time is different when we are dead from what it is when we are alive. In life, time moves in a chronological pattern of minutes, hours, days, weeks, months, and years. It is precise and forward moving. Death is a whole other story; one in which years can pass by like minutes, and we are able to revisit our past with clarity. While our earthly activities are all-consuming when we are alive in solid form, and we notice the microcosm of passing minutes, our spirit form is vast and eternal, hosting many incarnations and focusing on the macrocosm. Those minutes passed brushing our teeth are minuscule when we start thinking in the terms of multiple lifetimes.

Psychics and quantum physicists alike are now thinking in the parallel when contemplating time. What psychics once referred to solely as "past-life readings" is now more often being referred to as "parallel lives," as we begin to understand that lifetimes are happening simultaneously. This belief resembles the multidimensional theories of modern science.*

In my work as a psychic medium, I have also heard time and time again from spirits that time doesn't pass the same for them as it does for those of us still living, as the dead move through decades like we move through years. This is due in part to all the things they no longer have to experience, all the tedious little things we do every day, like brushing our teeth, eating, and sleeping.

The dead also have the ability to revisit moments in their life, viewing them from multiple perspectives. Those who passed with things unfinished and wounds unexplored revisit those moments to work out what caused the trouble and pain they experienced and how things could have gone differently. The dead are not limited to reviewing only the painful moments of their existence, they also spend time with the beautiful, loving, and exciting moments of their many incarnations. This reflectiveness is necessary for a soul to grow, and with that in mind, the space in which the dead exist is timeless, allowing souls the ability to reconnect wherever they need to in their time line.

The wobbliness of time also affects spirits' ability to move quickly between locations separated by large distances. In the

---

*I firmly believe this, and I have experienced reconnection to my own past/parallel lives in which this life that I am living as Salicrow is cross-pollinating with alternate lifetimes my soul is experiencing.

realm of the dead a spirit can move from space to space instantaneously, as they are not limited by the need to move a physical body. Those of us who have out-of-body experiences or practice journeywork understand this effortless movement and lack of time. While journeying I once traveled instantaneously from my home in Vermont to a hospital room in Sacramento, California, where my dad was sitting on the bed in a johnny. My spirit was in the upper corner of the room near the window, and he had his back to me. Within a moment of me realizing where I was, my father turned around and looked straight at me, and I was back in my body in a flash. Later my father (who was also psychic) told me that he thought I was an angel. There have also been times when my sisters and I all experienced a visitation from my great-grandmother within a few moments of one another, regardless of the fact that we live miles away from one another.

When seeking contact with our Beloved Dead it is important to remember the wobbliness of time and the grace that it allows us, as many people feel overwhelmed with guilt if they cannot be with their dead when they are crossing into spirit, or if they are unable to attend the funeral. This feeling of failure often becomes infused with the emotions of mourning and turns into a deep feeling that they have disappointed their loved one and are somehow unworthy of that spirit's love, something I believe is a misguided belief that comes out of our culture's fear and avoidance of death. This fear makes us distort our feelings of loss into one of deserved abandonment, treating death as if it were a conscious decision. In truth, the moments immediately following death involve the spirit of the recently departed traveling from place to place, connecting with the ones they love and those who love them.

🌿Exploring Wobbly Time

For those of you wanting to explore the idea of wobbly time I invite you to think about who you would visit if you were to die right now. If time and space were not barriers to your travel, who would you energetically be called to? Whom do you love? Whom do you have unfinished business with? Whom are you connected to in the web of humanity? Meditate or journey on this thought, imagining that you are visiting those people and how that visitation would feel. This is in many ways like the journey the soul takes when it is no longer connected to the body, and for some this connection and visitation happens in the months leading up to death as well.

3

SITTING WITH DEATH

Self Vigiling

ANNE-MARIE KEPPEL

Dare you crack the door
To your dying room?

To gaze upon
Shake out
Make poignant

The sour grudges
Unswum waters
and
Songs you didn't intend
To chain
　　Down

At this hour
with
Strength of pulse

Mind and tongue
To untangle
Wounds
Words
Woes

Dare you
Work
To darn
The holes
In the Comforter
Of your deathbed?

·····················✳·····················

THE GRAY

Through countless conversations with my clients' Beloved Dead, I have come to understand that after death we gather with our soul family—biological and chosen—and wait until the ones with whom we share connections have joined us in spirit before beginning the cycle of reincarnation together again. This cycle of waiting ensures that we always have loved ones there for us when our time comes. Just as the majority of us have family and friends eager for our arrival at birth, so, too, do we have loved ones waiting upon our death. When our time of crossing gets close, our Beloved Dead begin to gather around us, ready to welcome us home. This is why many people talk about seeing their mother, father, sisters, and husbands when they are in the process of dying. They are not imagining these visitations; they are real!

A few years ago, I experienced a remarkable example of a spirit coming to help their loved one cross into death. While doing a

Spirit Gallery at the Lake Morey Resort, in Fairlee, Vermont, one of the guests I called onstage was accompanied by her dead mother-in-law, who began telling me that her husband, the woman's father-in-law, was in "the Gray" and would soon be joining her in spirit. She told me that he was currently in a nursing home and that he had been seeing her a lot lately; something her living daughter-in-law confirmed. Knowing that her time for communicating was short, as the crowd was large and galleries focus on getting shorter messages through to as many people as possible, she quickly told me that she and her husband had been dancers in their leisure time and that they would be dancing together again soon. Again, the daughter-in-law confirmed that they had indeed been avid dancers.

The gallery was being held during the annual Ladies Retreat, and the next day the same woman came to find me where I was doing psychic readings. She told me her husband had just called her to say that the family had all gathered at the nursing home as his father was actively dying. This was a profound confirmation for her that her mother-in-law was indeed there in spirit. The story continued the next year, when I again did a Spirit Gallery at the Ladies Retreat. This time it was the granddaughter of the "dancing lady" spirit who sought me out. She wanted to let me know that her mother had shared the information that came through during her spirit session with the family the previous year, as her grandfather was actively dying, and that it had brought great relief to the family. They were particularly moved by the statement about dancing, as moments before he passed, as he lay mostly comatose in his bed, he had suddenly put his hands up in the air and started shuffling his feet. Remembering the message from spirit, the family immediately recognized that he was dancing with his wife—that their mother had come to take him home!

The Gray is a term given to me by my personal spirits many years ago to describe the time surrounding death, when the person is still living but cannot get better, and the time just after passing, when a spirit may be confused about what has just happened. I look at the Gray as being similar to pregnancy. Pregnancy gives the living physical notice that a new being is about to be born. In the Gray, as a person steps into death's embrace, they begin to show more tangibly in the realm of the dead; the closer they get to their passing, the more they solidify in spirit, notifying their Beloved Dead that they will soon be with them. When a person's life force begins to dwindle and there is no way of replenishing it, they step into the betwixt and between. Mediums also exist in the Gray, with their ability to see, hear, sense, and know in the world of spirit directly affecting how clearly they are visible in the world of spirit; the stronger the medium, the more tangible they are in the Gray.

The Gray is a transitional space in which the world of spirit and the world of the living are only separated by the thinnest of veils, and spirits are connected to them equally. As I mentioned earlier, just before they die, people in the Gray often experience visitations from their Beloved Dead. They also astrally project, dreaming of flying around their old neighborhood, revisiting places and remembering times of their life as if they had just happened. The Gray and its strong connection to both worlds allows the recently departed to attend their own funeral, and the time after death for most people is spent sitting with their loved ones as they mourn and rejoicing with their Beloved Dead that they have been reunited.

When a spirit tells me that someone they love is in the Gray, it means they generally have up to a year to live; however, it can be much shorter and occasionally longer. In the case of a shorter time before crossing, the communicating spirit will generally tell me how long they believe it will be. When it comes to a longer time, it is usually because the person in question is afraid of death, and the extra time gained is generally unpleasant for them and their family. The Gray is a place of healing and preparation. If you feel your loved one has slipped into the Gray, honor their transition, help them find peace with their passing, and listen when they say they are being visited by their Beloved Dead.

Another unusual effect of someone being in the Gray—on either side of the veil, living or dead—is that the people who are caring for them are also more likely to experience their Beloved Dead. This is because the person in the Gray is like a conduit or channel, allowing spirit to use their energy more easily, just as it does with a psychic medium, which makes it easier for spirits to become more tangible in the world of the living.

ENCOUNTERS WITH SPIRIT

Sitting with someone who is in the Gray, actively dying, is a powerful experience that often changes people's view of life. It is a time of great pain and sorrow, as we watch the life force slip from our loved one, and one of deep emotional connection, where we are open, vulnerable, and real! Many people who hold space for the dying speak of powerful moments of being aware of the eternal soul and feeling the peaceful presence of their Beloved Dead around them. It is here, when death is within our company— patiently waiting or hanging out after the fact—that most people have encounters with spirit.

Anyone who has seen the light go out in someone's eyes recognizes the moment of death instantaneously, as the soul's departure is noticeable! We do not need to wait for the body to become cold; we know it the moment it happens as it is accompanied by a feeling, a sense of departure. Nurses often open windows after patients pass, sometimes out of superstition, but more often because they feel the soul and want to help it move on.

When my father was dying, he was surrounded by his three daughters and his three oldest granddaughters. We sang to him and told stories of his valor and charm as he lay between us on a hospital bed, heavily sedated with morphine. This went on for a day and a half, while my husband sat vigil outside the door of the hospital room, honoring the fact that my father was a Vietnam vet. When the time of my father's death was upon us, I left the room, needing to get a breath of fresh air, as I could feel it like a high-pressure system moving in before a storm. Before we could go outside for a break, my niece ran out of the room saying, "Grandpa's dying!"

I rushed inside and knocked over the bowl of water we had set aside for washing his body after death. The spilled water on the floor reminded me of how I had seen my great-grandmother's death in the water overflowed onto the bathroom floor when I was a kid. I knew that was indeed the moment. His passing was quick from that point on, and I experienced it in a medium-trance state in which I was both a daughter mourning the loss of her father and a medium helping a soul to cross into spirit.

Shortly after his death, when the nurses were checking his vitals and doing the official bits to mark him as dead, my family went outside for a smoke break in his honor. My father was a lover of cigarette and cannabis smoking. We lit a joint in his honor and jested with him about how he better give us a good show; we wanted physical signs he had crossed over with ease. This was due in part to the fact that my father also had some ability as a medium and had been working actively toward his dying and understanding how to communicate between the worlds of the living and spirit in the months leading up to his death, when he was in the Gray.

When we returned to the room, my sisters and I, along with our daughters, went about preparing my father's body, washing and anointing him as we played his favorite music and cried. A few moments into this procedure, while Creedence Clearwater Revival played "Run through the Jungle," my dad's favorite song, we all saw him blow smoke out his mouth. His way of showing us he had received our offering of smoke. He also squeezed my daughter's hand as she was washing his. Over the course of the next few weeks following his death he turned a friend's windshield wipers on, moved my keys across the kitchen table, and showed us a dozen other physical manifestations.

In this time of the Gray, spirits are fueled by the remaining energy of their life and the emotional power put out by their family's mourning. For those who are opportunistic like my father, it is a chance to show off. For most it is a time of visitation in dreams, sightings out of the corner of our eyes, smells of our Beloved Dead, and unexpected moments of deep emotion connected to the dearly departed. Regardless of whether your messages are flashy or subtle, these efforts are a sign of how much our loved ones in spirit want us to know they are okay!

OUT-OF-BODY EXPERIENCES

As I mentioned earlier it is normal for people who are actively dying to have out-of-body experiences. When my grandfather was dying of cancer, I was going to visit him once a week, spending time with him and allowing my aunt to have time away. I was only twenty-four years old and a mother of two young children. While I had always been aware of spirits, holding space for someone I loved while they died was new to me, and I found it both intriguing and terrifying. I was afraid to say the wrong thing or do the wrong thing. I was afraid he would die when I was the only one there, and I was afraid because I knew deep down inside that death was going to become a regular part of my life. In truth, I had known this my whole life, as my childhood was filled with every death imaginable, from the long death of old age to mental illness, accidents, child death, and murder. I always knew I was being prepared, but it was my grandfather's death that brought that fact home!

Being my father's father, my grandfather came from the same family line that my gifts came from. While he was the son of Grammy Brown, my great-grandmother and first spiritual teacher, he had never displayed any signs of psychic ability, but in his dying that all changed. He began to dream of flying around the town of Whitefield, New Hampshire, where he had been part of the town crew for more than forty years. In his dreams he was traveling the roads he paved in the summer and plowed in the winter. My aunt and her husband didn't know what to do with this information and imagined it to be a sign that his mind was going. They laughed about it as a way to make light of a heavy situation, not understanding that he was having out-of-body experiences. When I heard of his dreams I knew where my place was in his dying. It was up to me to explain to him what was happening and what it meant for him.

I had had my first real out-of-body experience that I recognized as such a few years before, after giving birth to my daughter by cesarean. I was lying in the hospital bed in an extreme amount of pain, as I waited for the nurse to bring me pain medication, when I suddenly found myself in the upper right-hand corner of the room, looking down on my body in the bed and my husband standing beside me, changing our daughter's diaper. I felt no pain from this vantage point and through my studies knew what was happening to me; my soul had separated from my body. This moment in the hospital room was an instant knowing, a confirmation of my belief that the soul is eternal.

Remembering my own experience, I went into my grandfather's room and started a conversation with him about dying. I told him I had heard what he was dreaming of and that I believed that his experience was similar to the one I had after the birth of my daughter. I shared my story with him and watched as he let it sink in and accept it as truth.

A few weeks later Grammy Brown came to me in a dream and told me that I had to tell my grandfather that she was waiting for him and that he needed to let go, and she would come for him. His experiences of being out of his body helped him to accept what I was saying and know that he would be okay; his soul would go on, and he would see his beloved mother again. He died three days later.

Many people have out-of-body experiences without knowing it, experiencing a sense of traveling in their mind when journeying, dreaming, and utilizing the healing medicine of sacred plants such as cannabis, psilocybin, and ayahuasca. In these altered states of deep relaxation and trance we are more fluid, and the connection of our soul to our body is not as locked in. This experience is often sought out by those who seek personal confirmation that their soul and body are separate.

Many, however, never explore such a state while fully alive, fearing that their soul may lose its way and become permanently separated from the body, unable to return. This, however, is a needless worry, as our soul carries a connection to our body even when we are having such an experience. Psychic seers and mystics see the soul as being connected to the body by a silver cord. This cord is infinitely long, yet all we have to do is think of the cord and our desire to return to our body, and it will be so. The transaction is as immediate as that of our Beloved Dead, who can travel from visiting loved ones in Vermont to those in California in the blink of an eye.

While not all who are dying will have such an experience, it is common enough that I would have you know of it. It is also why my sister practiced journeywork with my father daily in the months leading up to his death; she was helping him become comfortable with being outside of his body. I have no doubt that this helped him cross into spirit, and I am even more sure that it gave him steady footing on what to expect when he died.

HEIGHTENED PSYCHIC PHENOMENON

Death is in many ways an energetic vortex, opening a portal into the world of spirit. It has an energy force all its own, and it often creates surges in psychic phenomenon. While spirit activity is by far the most common experience to happen in the presence of death, it is not unusual to also have uncanny moments of knowing or mind reading, particularly when the person dying is nonverbal, or to repeatedly notice number sequences such as 11:11, 1:11, and 2:22.

Seeing these number sequences—also known as master numbers—everywhere they look is common for many people. These moments are seldom random, as the master number sequences seen on clocks, phones, and street addresses often come when the recipient of the sign is thinking about something important, and when you have a loved one in the Gray, there is nothing more important!

If you are currently holding space for someone who is actively dying, and you are repeatedly experiencing the 11:11 phenomenon, take note of what you were thinking or doing in the moments before noticing the numbers, for these are "heads up, pay attention" moments in which our spirit guides and ancestors are getting our attention, making sure we realize the importance of that which we are doing or thinking. We look at the clock at that precise moment because doing so will make us see it as peculiar, and spirits are opportunistic. The act of making us look at the clock or our phone at that precise moment is done in the same way that they make us take note of the song playing on the radio that will remind us of them: they throw their energy at us!

Mind reading is a bit more advanced and only likely to happen to people who are more psychically sensitive. It happens most often when the dying person is nonverbal, or comatose, in which case they are unable to communicate their needs and feelings to those who stand vigil with them. In such cases the sensitive will find they simply know what their loved one needs, or what they want to say. They may find themselves expressing how they believe their dying loved one feels about others who are present in the room or feeling adamant about what their last wishes are. In most cases the mind-reading ability dissipates after death, as the recipient of the message was more open while sitting in the presence of someone who was in the Gray. However, having the experience shows that the person has psychic potential that they could develop with practice and technique.

Most common is a sense of being more aware, more alive, and more vulnerable and sensitive to sound, smell, and lighting. Any time we sit with death things get surreal, in the same way that being present during labor and delivery of a child does. I love these moments that in truth are similar to microdosing psilocybin or smoking certain strains of cannabis grown for clarity of mind. I compare them because I have experienced them all, and all are shamanic in nature, being doorways to the betwixt and between. Shamans, labor and birth workers, EMTs, death doulas, and mediums all thrive in this space, recognizing it as a time deeply connected to the universal life force, which while called by many names, is most often simply referred to as God! These people all fall into the category of seeker. They are those who want direct contact with the unknown and seek to help others find peace when it is their time to voyage into the great beyond.

Places of death, such as hospitals, graveyards, and highways with many fatal accidents, also carry this energy. For death creates portals there, shortcuts for high-traffic areas. These not only make it easier for people to experience the spirit world, but they also unfortunately have a tendency to call death to them more often, which explains why those highway grave markers seem to cluster. Nurses often experience spirits in the halls late at night, and mediums can't go to the grocery store without seeing a few dead people, for it is the way of death to be attracted to its stewards.

Whether your psychic experiences are limited to those moments of being near death or happen regularly after the loss of a loved one often depends on your natural ability. It's important to recognize that ability and skill are two different things. Ability is what we are born with; developed over previous lifetimes, it is the sum of what we are capable of. Most people never reach their full potential psychically due to lack of dedication. This is not meant to judge but more to point out that psychic skill is like any other skill: it takes time and hard work. Most people will not have the level of interest in psychic development necessary to push themselves. That's okay! We are not all meant to be the same. While some of us will draw from time to time or go to a "paint and sip" class with our friends, few of us have the desire, talent, and perseverance necessary to become true artists. Yet that should not keep us from the enjoyment of making art! Nor should we see our personal experiences with spirit as of no importance simply because they are fleeting.

4

DYING

Through the Door
POEM BY TRAVIS BARRETT
ILLUSTRATIONS BY SANDRA BARRETT (SANDYCROW)

Auntie Baba had known something was up,
And had wondered what the new day would bring.
So, when dawn arrived, she still was not up,
But was awoken by a gentle ring.

The family down the lane was worried,
Old Pops wouldn't rise from bed anymore.
So, Baba packed her bag and hurried
Down the lane, right to the family's door.

She gathered the family together
And consoled those that loved their dear Old Pops.
She opened her bag and like a feather,
Drifted lit candles and tea in their cups.

"We must all sing him through the final door,"
She said, and as Baba's voice rose and fell,
Unseen, arrived those who had gone before.
Said Auntie Baba, "Come and wish him well."

All the spirits in flesh and those without,
Gathered 'round him and wept and laughed and sung,
Remembered their love and gave a great shout,
And out of his body Old Pops was flung.

They cherished his love and memory
And although they were sad, they well knew
Their happy Old Pops was now truly free
And when the time came, he'd come for them, too.

CHANGING FOCUS

Over the years I have been called to many deathbeds, usually by a close friend who wants me to help ease the passage of their beloved parent. I have sat cross-legged next to friends' mothers, doing Reiki on them as they died from cancer, separated and mixed toxic concoctions into a glass of juice for a friend who ended her painful battle through Vermont's Death with Dignity act, and showed up like the angel of death to help a fellow Reiki master let go of the fight and find her way to the other side. Through these deaths I learned that even the brave and spiritual can get hung up in the process of dying!

My friend Jane lived long with her death. Battling cancer for years, she was a ray of light in a dark world. A Reiki master in her own right, she explored alternative options, as well as traditional medicine, and still the cancer never let go of its hold on her. After years of fighting the fight, she finally approached the end of the line, the point at which she realized that there was no other outcome from this than death. She recognized she was in the Gray and truly embraced the idea of her passing. But she was still scared—scared to leave the two boys she raised alone and scared to enter the unknown without having lived her life as fully as she had hoped. Thoughts of *What if?* plagued her mind: What if she had overlooked something? What if they needed her? These things kept her going long past the point where she had any quality of life. Her home was like a sanatorium, constantly being sterilized by any who attended her, as her immune system had been shit for months. She was only leaving it for the long arduous drive to the doctors, where she bundled up in layers and hid behind masks, hats, and sunglasses for her own safety. She knew she had to go, but she just couldn't.

On the day before Jane died, I was teaching a vocal toning class at the wellness center I owned, and one of people taking the class was my friend Jenn, who was also a Reiki master and a good friend of Jane's. After class she told me how she was going to go up and sit with Jane and her boys, as she felt that Jane's time was coming soon. She told me how in the last few days she had become mostly nonverbal and was only able to stay awake for short periods of time. I told her to give my best to Jane and headed home. Shortly after getting home, I became antsy, feeling like I couldn't sit still, like there was important business for me to be doing. I began packing my basket with sacred tools: rattles, incense, crystals, and other bits, called Jenn to tell her I was on my way down, and told my husband I would be going out, that I had a death to attend.

When I got there, Jenn greeted me at the door and introduced me to Jane's sons. The house was quiet, and you could feel that an aura of death had settled on the home. I went into Jane's room where she lay unconscious and spoke softly to her, saying, "I am here to help you cross over, Jane. There is nothing to fear." I looked around her room, seeing pictures of her sons and trinkets of her life. The lavender spray on her night stand, a Reiki table in the corner ready to be set up should she need it, and appointment cards on the dresser for her next doctor's visit.

I went into the living room and spoke with her sons for a while, asking them to gather photographs of people Jane loved who were dead. They came back with photos of their grandmother and other relatives, as well as photos from Jane's home country (she was from the U.K.). I then instructed them to remove the photos of themselves from her room and to replace them with photos of her mother and the other Beloved Dead who were waiting for her.

Jane died that night, not simply because we changed out the

photos, but that did play a part. It gave her something different to focus on when she opened her eyes periodically to connect to the world. Instead of seeing pictures of her sons, which made her want to rally and stay alive, she saw photos of the people who were waiting to welcome her. The fact that her sons were the ones who changed the pictures out was also important, as they changed the energy of the space, encouraging their mother to let go and join her loved ones in spirit.

When a person is struggling to let go, staying in a body that cannot heal, it is helpful for us to change their focal point. This is something I often recommend to people who have family members in nursing homes and hospices who are really just holding on out of fear. This fear is not always just fear of the afterlife and what will become of their spirit, it is also fear of leaving behind the ones you love. The photos we put up in their room for them to look at every day showing their grandchildren and great-grandchildren, weddings and babies, are reminders of life and what they leave behind in their passing. For some this creates an overwhelming desire to stay the course, so others do not need to mourn us. When we change the photos out, moving pictures of their Beloved Dead to the forefront of their vision, we not only show them what they are moving toward, we energetically give them our permission to go. Much like a parent preparing their child for a long stay at Grandma's talks about how fun it will be and shows them lots of photos of Grandma and her house to get them excited, we want to give our dying something to look forward to!

Do not worry that they might feel abandoned by you if you change out the photos. You can still have pictures of the living family in the room, just move them out of their immediate vision. When you go to visit, talk about the ones they are joining and how happy the family is that they will finally be reunited with the ones they have lost. Make death something that feels comfortable and natural, something to celebrate and hold vigil for, just as we do with birth!

ENERGETIC LOCKS

There are places in the body where a soul can get stuck; places like ankles and wrists, hips and heart that keep us connected to the physical world. It is often these points that hold our spirit to our body, locked in place by memories of doing and being. Our hips and buttocks remind us we are grounded in the physical, our wrists and ankles remind us of all the things we have done manually: the miles we have walked, the blankets we have crocheted, the children we have held and bathed, the letters we have written, and the hours we have stood in line. Our heart holds us here with love; love for our family and friends, love for our life purpose, and love for the land we live on and the community we are part of. In dying, it is usually these places in the body that we receive the most resistance from, as they hold the memories of the life we have lived.

While it is common for people to have out-of-body experiences when they are dying, they are often jolted back into their body when their consciousness believes it has drifted too far. The fear is seldom well thought out; instead it is an impulsive reaction, a moment in which the soul feels the fear of getting lost or being unable to return to the ones they love, and it is through these locks that they snap themselves back in, holding on through the memory of living, even if their experience of life is far from good.

When assisting someone who is actively dying, helping them to loosen these locks is helpful as it allows them to realize that they can overcome the knee-jerk reaction to jump back into the body.

My sister spent many hours working on this with my father in the months leading up to his death. While he believed himself comfortable with the idea of dying, he knew he was a fighter and didn't want to struggle to overcome his auto-pilot programming.

While not everyone has loved ones who are into spiritual exploration, everyone becomes more curious about the spirit when they are sitting with their own mortality. You will be surprised at who will be willing to learn when they are being courted by death!

Below I have included a guided meditation you can use while working with the dying, whether it be another or yourself. If you are doing this for yourself, I suggest that you read it through a few times, then record yourself reading it. This will allow you to listen to it from the fluid, relaxed state of a light trance instead of engaging your analytical mind to read.

🌿Meditation for Releasing Body Locks

Make sure that the recipient is comfortable and warm and in as little pain as possible and begin reading the meditation below at a slow, even pace.

⌒

Begin by placing your focus on your breathing, allowing yourself to breathe as deeply as you can, following your breath as it fills and empties from your lungs. Imagine that with each breath in you are feeding your spirit, and with each breath out you are releasing pain, fear, and uncertainty.

Continue to breathe as you bring your consciousness to your right ankle. Move your ankle around a bit if you can, making small circles in a counterclockwise direction. If you are unable to move your feet, imagine that you are doing so by visualizing it in your mind. Continue to breathe, making small circles as you do. Imagine that you are unscrewing something tight, like the top of a jar or a screw. Do this for a few moments, allowing your mind to wander as it will, coming back to your ankle on every inhale. Make note of feelings and memories that come up when you do, noting that the right side of the body is associated with the paternal side of our family and the masculine, doing side of our mind.

Take a deep breath in and move your focus to your left ankle. Begin to move your left foot in a counterclockwise motion, again imagine that you are unscrewing something, releasing the tightness that holds it in place. Pay attention to any thoughts, feelings, or old memories that present themselves. Do this for a few moments as you allow your mind to wander, knowing that the left side of our body is connected to the maternal side of our family and the receptive part of our nature.

Now move both ankles together in a counterclockwise motion and imagine them getting loose. If you are feeling too tired to do this physically, just follow along with the sound of my voice and imagine you are unscrewing or loosening the locks of your ankles. Give thanks for all the miles you have walked and the moments of your life that were filled with dancing, hiking, and moving about as you do.

Taking a few deep breaths and move your attention to your pelvis, focusing on your hip joints. Imagine there is a screw in the side of your right hip, or a pressure-relief valve. Begin unwinding it in your mind, focusing on a counterclockwise motion. If strong emotions come up simply breathe through them, noting that again you are connecting to your paternal/masculine side. Breathe deeply and give thanks as emotions come up, releasing them into the ether.

Move to the left hip and connect to the maternal, feminine side of your body. Begin to imagine that counterclockwise rotation opening or releasing your left hip. Take deep breaths in and out and give thanks to any emotions and memories that come up. Note that you are actively giving thanks for the life you have lived, while simultaneously releasing the pain of your story that keeps you stuck in this body.

With every breath your body is more relaxed. With every breath you feel your soul becoming buoyant, loose, and less encumbered. If you feel resistance at any point breathe into it, allow the feelings to come, do not resist! Spend a few minutes now focusing on both of your hips, remembering all the pleasure and stability they have provided you. Give thanks for their security and exhale deeply.

Move up your body and take time to breathe as you make your way up your spine, releasing any pressure you have in your lower back and stomach. Continuing to breathe, move up into your heart chakra, the energy center in the middle of your chest. This is the place where love resides. Breathe deeply as you think of all the living people who love you, allowing yourself to take a few moments here, breathing in . . . and out . . . in . . . and out. Now imagine there is a valve in the center of that chakra, and like a lid on a jar, begin to open it by spinning it counterclockwise. Do not be surprised if you find emotions coming to the surface. Do not hold back these emotions; allow tears to come if they must. Now imagine there is a soft pink light emanating from your heart chakra. With the valve open you can see the light seeping out. Breathe deeply and imagine that light stretching out to reach for those you love who have crossed into spirit before you. Like a gossamer rope it extends out of your heart toward your Beloved Dead. Note the appearance of any visitors, spirits who may be holding space, waiting for you to join them on the other side.

You will begin to feel a lightness in your body as if you are floating just above it. Look down at your body and see that you are still attached at the wrists. Focus first on your right wrist and begin the act of unwinding, just as you have already done for your ankles, hips, and heart. Breathe deeply and begin to unscrew the hold on your right wrist in a counterclockwise motion, noting that this again holds a connection to the paternal/controlling side of your consciousness and that our hands and wrists represent control. In your mind give yourself permission to release control, noting any resistance and memories that come forward to be examined.

Now move to your left wrist, repeating the motion of unscrewing it in a counterclockwise motion as you breathe fully. Note again that the left side of our body holds our maternal/receptive side of our consciousness, and our left wrist often holds memories of the things that were out of our control, the things that happened to us. Breathe deeply and forgive yourself for the things you could not control. Again, breathe deeply, this time forgiving those who hurt you or left you feeling as if you were helpless.

With your body's locks now opened, imagine that your soul is now so buoyant that it floats to the ceiling of the room. Continue to breathe and notice how good it feels to be free of your body. Note any colors, shapes, sounds, smells, or thoughts that come to mind, as well as any spiritual visitors who have come to see you. If you have done this exercise before, allow yourself to move farther out, up through the ceiling or out the window into the yard. Continue to breathe and allow your soul to explore its newfound freedom.

I recommend leaving off at this point, allowing the dying to stay in the deeply relaxed state of trance or sleep. Note that this exercise works best if you do it often, as it prepares the soul for departure by loosening the locks and giving an instructional guide for leaving the body at death. After all, practicing for death is no different from doing Lamaze to prepare for birth. Just as mothers who practice breathing and body postures prior to labor have an easier go of it, so do those who practice leaving their body for death!

SOME DIE ALONE

During the second year of my Druid training we explored our own death by doing deep meditations around our passing. Meant to prepare us for a night of sleeping in our own grave, this particular exercise is very powerful as most people have never looked at their mortality under such a powerful lens. While I enjoyed the exercise, sitting with death was by no means a new thing for me.

During the meditation we were asked to first imagine that we had been given a year to live. After journeying with that thought for a while, the time line was moved to one month, then one day, and then our final moments. We were asked to imagine what that could look like, how we would want to experience it, who would be waiting for us, and who would be sitting by our bedside as we transitioned into spirit. While most of us had similar experiences of being surrounded by loved ones, my friend Rich imagined himself curled up in the woods at the root of a tree like an old dog who goes into the woods to die alone. Hearing how he saw himself dying caused a bit of distress for one or two of the people who were feeling sorry that he would have to die alone, but he went on to explain that it wasn't because he had to, it was because he wanted to!

While my vision was one of being surrounded by friends and family, I understood what he was talking about, as I had experienced the same thinking from some of the spirits with whom I had communicated. These were people who couldn't seem to die when anyone was watching, preferring to be alone when they left this world. Grammy Brown was one of those! She died in the hospital twenty minutes before we got there. I was so hurt and so confused and felt so guilty! I was only twelve years old, and I couldn't understand her desire for privacy, but as I listened to spirit after spirit tell me their stories, I understood that the reasoning had to do with their own feelings of guilt. If their family were in the room with them, they would hold on for all they were worth, not wanting to see their loved ones suffer at their passing.

One of the common things I hear from the living when they come for a spirit communication session is that they feel guilty about not being there when their loved one was passing, as if they had failed somehow in their duty. This guilt is often a way for them to transfer the pain of loss that they feel, allowing them to focus instead on what a failure they were and if they had only done better things would have been different, instead of realizing they had absolutely nothing to do with it. In most of these cases the spirit with whom they are seeking connection is already aware of their guilt and mentions it before they do. I often find myself saying, "You were unable to say good-bye" or "They left moments after you left the room," as their Beloved Dead is aware of their pain over missing the momentous moment. The next thing I say is almost always, "They waited for you to leave the room before they let go" or "They want you to know they couldn't die with someone watching them."

We need to remember that death is personal and that it is about the person who is crossing over. Regardless of the ripple effect it has on the living, the decisions should ultimately be focused on what the spirit departing needs. If your loved one leaves moments after you leave the room or while you are still making a mad dash across the state to get to the hospital, know that it was what was best for them and remember that time is wobbly. They know how much you love them, they know you wanted to be there, they know you feel guilty and torn over not being able to say good-bye. While they needed to depart in a manner that was best for them, they do generally apologize for not being able to say good-bye.

If you have experienced the loss of a loved one without being able to say good-bye—regardless if you were just outside the door or across the world—they know how you feel! Remember that spirit is not limited by time or space. Speak your words out loud, tell them how much you love them and miss them, cry for them, toast them, and smoke for them, honoring them in the best way you see fit. It is normal to have a relationship with our Beloved Dead; our souls do not stop being connected simply because someone dies.

DEATH WITH DIGNITY

My friend Briga was the third person in the state of Vermont to cross into spirit using the Death with Dignity act (the Patient Choice and Control at End of Life Act/Act 39). After a long battle with terminal cancer she decided that she no longer wanted to suffer. It was not an easy decision to make, nor was it easy to gain access to the act. To do so she needed to prove that she was making the decision in her right mind and provide character witnesses that supported this truth. I was one of the people who signed, saying she was making her decision from a place of clarity and certainty. I was honored and amazed to take part in such a death and gave thanks for Dr. Kevorkian's groundbreaking work in the field.

Having watched people struggle and suffer through long deaths, and having witnessed the ease and beauty of my friend Briga's passing, I have no hesitation in saying that the Death with Dignity act is a good thing and the right death for some people. From a spiritual perspective I would add that a death such as this is a totally different experience from one where someone takes their own life due to depression and hopelessness. Where the person who dies from emotional wounding and despair is often put in a space of deep healing that I refer to as "Time Out" (see chapter 6), those who die through euthanasia experience a crossing similar to those who die of natural causes. It is my hope that in sharing Briga's story, others will be able to see the beauty in this path.

BRIGA AND THE GOOD DEATH

Briga walked to her death like a warrior queen! She woke the house early Sunday morning announcing she was done, after spending the wee hours of the morning writing love letters to friends and family who were not present. Within moments of announcing her decision to take the medicine, we began the preparation for plan B: the Patient Choice and Control at End of Life Act (Act 39), which provides Vermont residents with a terminal disease the option of being prescribed medication to hasten the end of their life. We had already tried plan A, a weekend of energy work with her closest friends and family in which we tried to help her pass naturally.

The house was alert and moving within moments, as we had mentally prepared for this possibility all weekend. We created sacred space in Briga's living room, lighting candles and setting up a temporary altar and smoking the space with herbs and incense before preparing the medication. The medication was a two-part process: the first elixir was intended to settle the stomach, ensuring that the patient could keep down the toxic slurry that was to follow thirty minutes later. As we gloved up and separated pills, Briga prepared herself, dressing in purples and blues and draping her shoulders with the wrap she had worn at countless ceremonies and fires. It was a deep, clear moment but by no means was it stagnant or humorless, for Briga was neither!

While the second medication was being prepared, Briga took the first. Knowing we had thirty minutes before she left the world of the living, we gathered together outside her bedroom, taking photos, hugging, and crying. Briga embraced each of us in turn, infusing each hug with love that was meant to last a lifetime. In truth, the medication was true to its timing, but sitting in death's waiting room, the thirty minutes of time simultaneously felt like it lasted forever and was over in the blink of an eye.

When Briga began to get drowsy we moved into her bedroom. Briga was helped into her bed where she was surrounded by her brother on one side, our Druid teacher Ivan on the other, and the rest of us gathered in where we could. The room had already been prepared with candles, crystals, and flowers, and the weight of imminent death sat heavy in the space. We then began to sing! In many ways it was one of the most beautiful deaths I have ever experienced. She left her body as if going to sleep, dozing off with a smile on her face and in the warm embrace of those who loved her.

The most remarkable part came after her crossing, for it was here that the difference between a suicide and the end-of-life choice were made clear to me: Briga was speaking to me within ten minutes of her death, giving me instructions to get tea and coffee on and snacks out for the people who would be arriving for her wake! This clearly separated her death from that of a suicide, as she was not at all disoriented and did not need to process the trauma of her passing. Her experience was that of a well-adjusted soul dying from natural causes!

I understand that this is not something with which everyone will feel comfortable. That being said, we consider euthanasia an acceptable and humane end of life when our animals are suffering. Having watched more than one person struggle to breathe and struggle to die, with heavy doses of pain medication clouding their mind and limiting their ability to communicate, I can honestly say that the Death with Dignity act is a blessing.

5

DEATH

IN MY OPINION, Americans sterilized death in the 1950s, standardizing the mourning period into a wake, a funeral, and two weeks of casseroles and then expecting us to move on with our lives. This homogenized view of death has been enforced by the transference of death care from the family-home environment to the hospital. While some of us have no choice but to die in a hospital, when given the choice, the option of dying at home is generally found to be more healing for the family, as home is not sterile and devoid of emotion but instead filled with love!

When my great-grandmother died, I was twelve years old and had little say about how her body was cared for or what we were supposed to do. In fact, I didn't know much about the physical workings of death or its aftercare. As I mentioned earlier, she died in a hospital twenty minutes before any of her family arrived, choosing to die alone so as not to be held back by those of us who would have been begging her not to go.

When I went into the hospital room to view her body, it felt wrong! The room was empty of color, empty of light, empty of anything personal or real, and there she lay, alone. She had been a colorful woman, her life made up of bold-colored quilts, painted flowers, and mismatched dishes. Her body lying in a sterile hospital room seemed to hold nothing of her at all. The hospital lacked the distinguishing smells of life, replacing her personal scent of Miss Breck hairspray and cigarettes with the harsh odor of cleaners and medicated rubs. We spent a few moments with her body and then left to mourn as a family in her home, where we could feel her closeness. The next time I saw my great-grandmother's body was days later, when she was lying in her coffin.

SITTING WITH THE DEAD

The traditional mourning practice of sitting with the dead is known as a wake. Over the years wakes have changed greatly. What in modern times we see as visiting hours at the funeral home, which take place when the body has been properly prepared through embalming or cremation, was once the three days following a death in which family and friends would sit with the dead, holding space and giving honor. The practice is believed to have originated in Celtic Ireland and adopted by the Catholic faith as a way of offering protection from evil spirits. In traditional fashion, those who sit with the dead stay awake all night keeping guard.

When I learned of this tradition, I suddenly understood what had felt wrong about the process following my great-grandmother's death: no one had sat with her, not even for an hour. In our dysphoria we were overcome with emotion and unable to release it or understand it in the environment of the hospital, as we needed to find comfort in the sights and smells provided by her home. I understood immediately the value of a wake, whether it be a full three days of vigilant guard or an hour or two of deep conversation.

Most hospitals understand the needs of the family surrounding death and are considerate, allowing time for mourning in which it is possible to sit with our dead. They understand that many people need to see, touch, and talk to their Beloved Dead before they can accept that the person has actually passed and respect that people have a variety of spiritual and religious beliefs, all with deep regard for the process of death. While we may not be able to spend three days in the hospital room, we are often allotted a couple of hours to say our good-byes and prepare the body of our beloved in what way feels best for the needs of the dead and our family.

If our loved ones are fortunate enough to die in a home setting, we have the opportunity to truly sit with their body as their spirit crosses the veil, and some have the ability to sit for the full three days. While we may no longer feel the need to protect the dead or ourselves from malign spirits, having time in which to say good-bye and grieve while in the presence of a loved one's body is good for both the living and the dead. While the dead can travel instantly to any location to experience how much they will be mourned, there is something sacred about their body that keeps them loosely attached for the first few days. There is also something truly powerful about sitting with the dead that allows the living to tangibly understand death. And for the sensitive, the experience provides an opportunity to feel that their loved one still exists outside of that body.

Few of us will have the opportunity to be part of a true wake in which we sit with the body for three days. I have been part of such an experience twice, as both my friend Briga and my Druid teacher Ivan had traditional wakes in which their bodies were tended by living loved ones holding space for three days. It is a powerful process that affects all those who take part in it, for sitting with death makes us reflect on our own mortality as well as the life of the one with whom we are sitting.

While I understand and respect the logical need to care for the body after death in terms of embalming and cremation, I would like to point out that there are other options. In some states, like Vermont, people are allowed to transport the bodies of loved ones for cremation themselves, and green burials are becoming more and more common. When exploring options for our body or that of a loved one, it is worth looking into alternative possibilities, making sure we know the legal regulations of the state we live in.

HONORING AND ANOINTING

My father died in the intensive care unit of the Marlborough hospital in Marlborough, Massachusetts, which was quite ironic actually, as he had smoked Marlboro cigarettes most of his life. While he technically died of complications from coming in contact with Agent Orange during his service in Vietnam, I am sure his love of tobacco played a part in his story.

Although he had been preparing for his death for more than a year, the acute, sitting-with-death part of his story began at the winter solstice of 2012 and ended the twenty-seventh of December. He went into the hospital Christmas evening. My sister Sandy went down that evening to see how bad he was, and I waited up north as I had an appointment the following morning to get my cracked windshield replaced, which I really didn't want to miss. The appointment was in the early morning, and by the time my windshield was done, Grammy Brown was instructing me to get on the road and bring my father's flag.

The flag in question was one my father had carried throughout most of his time in Vietnam, sending it home to my great-grandmother weeks before he was in a battle that left him 100 percent disabled, with a glass eye and shrapnel in his brain. The flag in many ways was a symbol of his life and service, and it had hung on display in our house as a child. I knew by her asking me to bring it that she was saying he was finally coming home to her, crossing the veil into spirit.

His active dying took about two days; something I spoke of earlier in the book. It was a deeply sacred experience, and it did not end with his death, for we the living still had work to do. My sister Sandy and I had long been working with death by the time my father's passing came: I as a psychic medium, and Sandy as a minister performing funerals for families. Both of us were also unofficial doulas. With each death we encountered we had delved deeper into the sacred art of death care and the importance of ritual ceremonies to honor the dead—one of the most important being the honoring and anointing of the body after death.

Active dying is truly different in every case, but after death there are things that happen to the body that are pretty much universal. These things may be startling the first time you experience them, but they are truly a natural part of the process. Upon death the heart stops and the eyes cloud over, making it easy to see how the eyes are considered the doorway to the soul. Shortly after death the body may twitch a bit as the nervous system shuts down. All the while rigor mortis is setting in, which may make the body begin to stiffen. If your loved one had a pacemaker it will keep ticking for a few minutes after death. With the release of life, it is normal for the body to purge, which can come in the form of defecating, urinating, or purging from the mouth. As blood is no longer circulating through the body it will start pooling under the skin, turning it purple in blotches. While these things may not be pretty, there is a beauty to standing present with death that makes even these things sacred. The dead are close by as their bodies are tended, making it truly an honor to hold this vigil.

Regardless of the fact that my father had died in a hospital, we performed the sacred act of washing and oiling his body ourselves. Simply asking the nurses for a bowl of warm water, towels, and washcloths, we established our spiritual right to care for our dead. This is something we all can do; we have a right to care for our loved ones in the way that is in accordance with our spiritual and religious beliefs. If you are denied the right to do so, please make sure you explain to them that this is a spiritual/religious belief of yours, and they will quickly see your side of the story more favorably. (Most hospitals will allow this unless there is risk of contagion.) The Marlborough hospital was gracious and respectful, giving us as much time as we needed and supplying us with ample hot water and towels.

After taking a moment outside to gather ourselves, we returned to my father's room to perform the care of his body. We had brought fragrant soap and oils with us from home and a music playlist of his favorite songs to play while we washed and anointed him. The six of us—my two sisters and our eldest daughters—lovingly washed my father's body, cleaning away the struggle of dying. We could feel his presence with us strongly, noticing the signs he gave us that he was there, like smoke coming from his mouth, the clasping of my daughter's hand, and the wink of his glass eye. We wet down his hair and combed it and the handlebar mustache that he was so proud of. We then began oiling his body with fragrant oils. We did so not only as his daughters and granddaughters but also as priestesses performing the most important ritual of all: helping him to step more fully into spirit as we showed love and respect for his body, with its three belly buttons (two of which were really bullet holes) and the scar on his chest where it had been cut open for a pacemaker years ago. He loved this attention and honoring, particularly as he was a bit of a dandy and always wanted to look his best.

After we had finished the ceremony of preparing his body, one of the nurses from the ICU came in to talk to us. She told us that she was not sure what we had been doing, but for the hour and a half we were caring for our father not a single alarm had gone off in the ICU, something she found remarkable. She and the other nurses were touched by the way we cared for our dead, and they asked a lot of questions and shared some of the things they did to give honor to those who had crossed over.

Don't worry about whether you know how to do this; there is no right way or wrong way, no special oils or ointments needed. You can use their favorite soap, their favorite perfumes and oils, and in truth you can use what the hospital supplies or what you can pick up at the local pharmacy if you are in a pinch. The important part is the intention, the act of caring for your dead yourself, the honoring and acknowledging that they were special. Like the gentle washing of a newborn baby, the washing and anointing of our Beloved Dead is soft and loving. It is a chance to connect with your loved one through their body one final time.

If you are dying or someone you know is in the Gray, planning for their aftercare is a way of seeing the death as sacred and beautiful. Imagining how we will honor them or how we wish to be honored gives us an understanding that the end of physical life can be sacred, beautiful, and filled with love. It is also a way of connecting to the eternal presence of death, which we all will embrace at some point. I myself want to be washed in rose water and oiled in fragrant, musky oils. I want to cross into spirit as a priestess!

GREETED BY LOVED ONES

Death is a time of rejoicing for those in spirit! Just as we celebrate the birth of a child, the dead welcome their loved ones home with joy. As I mentioned earlier, as a dying soul steps into the Gray, they become more visible to their loved ones in spirit. During a person's time in the Gray their Beloved Dead draw closer to them, and those closest prepare to welcome their loved one when their time of death comes.

I would like to say that everyone has someone come for them immediately after death, but that is simply not true. What is true is that while most of us have loved ones waiting for us, occasionally someone who is very traumatized or who has caused great harm to others may experience a time of confusion upon death, in which they are in limbo, stuck between consciousnesses, unaware they are dead. This does not happen often, but it is my opinion that this is what causes hauntings.

The great majority of us, however, are greeted by our Beloved Dead. Most people experience one or two spirits who first come to greet them; generally, those closest to them, such as their mother, husband, child, or best friend. Those of us who have lost a spouse or child are likely to find them waiting for us when we cross into the world of spirit. This reunion comes with potency, allowing us to realize we have crossed the threshold, no longer able to return to our body and the life we left behind. It is also a tender reunion time as we are still closely tied to the feeling of being alive and, straddling the line of betwixt and between, we feel more acutely, allowing us and the Beloved Dead who greet us to have a moment of tangible feeling.

Among those who greet the newly dead is the family's Wisdom

Keeper, the spiritual matriarch or patriarch who holds the family together, doing in death what they did in life! Wisdom Keepers collect the family dead. They hold their position on the other side until all of the loved ones they watch over have crossed into spirit or until another family Wisdom Keeper has come to replace them.

My family Wisdom Keeper is Grammy Brown, my paternal great-grandmother. She has held the role in my family since 1984 and is among the spirits who greet my family members upon their death. She will hold this position until my sister Sandy or I die. While she does not gather the souls of all of the family, she gathers those who had been under her watch, as well as any family members who have no personal dead to greet them.

While a family Wisdom Keeper does not need to be psychic, those who serve death as mediums or death doulas and those who find themselves present at all the family deaths are likely to end up with the role; hence, Sandy or I replacing our great-grandmother. A familiarity with the betwixt and between is helpful, as such spirits often begin making appearances to those in the dying process.

Our arrival in spirit is generally an experience of opening. Greeted first by the spirits closest to us, and/or the family Wisdom Keeper, we are gradually connected to other family members over time. In the days closest to our death, we are most often accompanied by only the few closest to us so as to not take away from the experience of mourning taking place with the living we have left behind. Spirits who have trauma at their time of death generally continue with this limited connection to spirits until they have processed their life's path.

Who in your family do you think holds the position of Wisdom Keeper in the spirit world? Can you think of a grandmother, father, aunt, or cousin whose kindness and generosity put everyone at ease and made everyone feel special? We all have someone in our family tree who plays this part in death. Creating a connection with that spirit while still alive is a great way to make the process of dying easier. This is something I do when helping people to cross; I look for their Wisdom Keeper and help them to understand that this spirit whom they love and trust will be ready to guide them as soon as they cross the threshold!

SPIRIT VISITATION

Death is miraculous! During the process of dying and shortly after death, when the veil between the worlds is thin, the newly dead are able to visit their living loved ones more easily, allowing them to connect in small ways with those they left behind. From dream visitations to phantom smells and songs on the radio, I experience more reports of contact with the dead in the days following their passing than at any other time. As I discussed earlier, I believe this is because when the spirit crosses the veil they create a power surge in the energetic field similar to that created by an Earth vortex or a medium. This allows more energy to be utilized by the spirit, making them more tangible in the world of the living and allowing those so inclined to reach out and say good-bye to the ones they are leaving behind. For most spirits this period of heightened energy and contact lasts only a short time, with the most potent times of contact being within the first three days.

My first real experience of such a visitation happened when I was in high school. While I had experienced spirit contact since early childhood, the only death I had personally experienced at that point was my great-grandmother's, which left me emotionally distraught and unable to perceive her communication. I was seventeen when my friend John committed suicide, jumping from a bridge just before Thanksgiving. While hindsight can point to his inevitable decision, at the time it was a shocking blow. He was a wonderful human being, with a kind heart, who was loved by many.

Psychically the night was charged, the air filled with an unpleasant essence of chaos and what I would later discover was sorrow. After finding out he had passed, a number of synchronicities became apparent, as I realized that things said in jest were really precognitive knowledge disguised in bad humor. That night when I lay in my bed, drifting off to sleep, I was awakened by someone standing in the middle of my room. At first, I thought my sister had gotten up to use the bathroom, but I soon realized the being wasn't living and that the person standing in my room was John. He didn't stay long, but in the time he was there I understood that he was alright, that regardless of what popular religious jargon said on the subject, he had not damned his soul by taking his life. I saw his pain sitting on him; pain from the life that had felt too heavy a burden and pain from the knowledge he carried of how his actions had hurt those who loved him. In the days following, attending his funeral and the private gathering of friends in his honor, I heard from various others how they had dreamed of John or that they had felt him while sitting in their car or thought they heard his laugh from across the room. These people I spoke to were not highly spiritual seekers that I knew of, but still they experienced visitation.

When we are deeply mourning, our pain is often so intense that we unintentionally create a hardening of our aura (energetic body), thus making it impossible for us to receive messages from our Beloved Dead. Clever spirits will try to reach those around us to get messages through during this time, which explains why our coworker can see our husband's spirit but we can't. While this can be frustrating, be thankful that your loved one is trying so hard to reach you and set up an altar where you can visit with them regularly. Doing so and speaking their name out loud helps us to release the shield we have placed around us.

Spirit communication is not limited to this time of betwixt and between surrounding death, but it is the time when it is most prolific.

6

THE SPIRIT WORLD

Twice Grieved

BARBARA WIGGETT BAUMANN

Estranged before his final breath
My brother is my friend in death
A blood bond weakened years ago
Has found a way to ebb and flow

His ways his own; misunderstood
His travels vast; 'twas bad or good?
I wondered why and grieved the loss
For years before his spirit crossed

As he adventured, I dug roots
We didn't know each other's truths
I wondered, "Does he think of me?"
But boundaries set, I let him be

Through miles and years, just empty space
No talks, no laughs, no ties, no grace

Then, suddenly, my heart was clenched
My soul knew that a life was quenched

A panicked, painful, mystery feeling
Foretold the call that sent me reeling
A bond, once broken, pierced my heart
The tales began to fall apart

Connection severed years ago
Left me with an empty hole
No time, no space, an astral place
He came to visit, face-to-face

In sacred space where dwell the wise
He conveyed our father's eyes
In him, in me, the family line
Where love and healing know no time

✳

CANDLELIGHT

The dead often describe the living in terms of luminosity, stating that they are attracted to the light of their living loved ones. We are all luminous to our Beloved Dead, drawing them in like a moth to a flame! Most people are like tealights, giving off a soft glow of light that can only be seen by those who are looking for us. However, those with the natural ability to communicate with the spirit world give off more light, with skilled mediums giving off a light radius similar to a lighthouse, drawing in spirits from far and near.

While everyone has the ability to connect with their Beloved

Dead, the potential level of skill varies between individuals. Generally speaking, those who experience spirit contact spontaneously throughout their life, having multiple episodes that are likely not limited to personal relations, have developed some level of skill in spirit communication in previous lifetimes. This means they are more likely to develop real skill than those who have had little to no spontaneous communication. I often compare spirit communication to art, stating that everyone can do art, but not everyone will be an artist. With this in mind, be careful not to compare your experience to others'.

For those who have had such experiences, I recommend beginning your spirit-communication development by first addressing your personal wounding. We all have finite energy as human beings, and this energy can get clogged up by old wounding that shows up as blocks in the chakras (energy centers) related to the trauma. Healing ourselves clears away the blocks, allowing more energy to move through our energetic system, which provides more "electricity" for the spirits to use in communication.

For those who have had little to no spontaneous contact, spirit communication can seem daunting. I will remind you here that we all give off light that attracts our Beloved Dead, which means some level of contact is available to us all! However, it is advisable to have realistic goals in your communication so that you do not cause yourself unneeded feelings of failure. Remember, spirit communication is something developed over lifetimes. The effort you put in now will pay off in this life and others.

Repetition and ritual can help to increase your spiritual light. Setting aside space and time for connecting with your Beloved Dead creates a sacred pattern between you and your loved ones. Each time we do so strengthens our commitment and dedication to connection. When we gather with others in remembrance of our Beloved Dead, it is likely that at least one person will have some kind of contact, as our tealight luminosity combined is greater than what we put out alone.

I often use the symbolism of a tealight to represent the light that the living gives off in the darkness, light that helps their Beloved Dead find and connect with them. Lighting a candle on our altar regularly is like leaving the outside light on for company; it's an invitation to visit. The repetition of the act becomes ritualistic, strengthening our connection to our loved ones in spirit and making personal contact more likely. Over time we will find that we are not only more sensitive to their personal communication methods but also to spirit contact in general.

When working on enhancing your ability to perceive spirit, it is helpful to keep the words *maybe, kind of,* and *I think so* out of your vocabulary when speaking of possible contact. These are phrases people often use to write off their experiences as coincidence. Saying the statement in an affirmative way (i.e., "I felt my father just now") instead of in a questioning manner (i.e., "I think I just felt my father") gives us the opportunity to feel out the truth. By taking the doubt out of our conversation we are forcing ourselves to feel in our body whether our experience was real. It generally is!

TWO-WAY POLICE MIRROR

Spirit communication is not an equal exchange. In fact, it is much easier for the dead to perceive us than it is for us to perceive them. I often use the analogy of a two-way mirror in a police interrogation room to explain how communication is experienced on either side of the veil. In this analogy the spirits are on the police side of the mirror, and we, the living, are on the side being observed. This does not mean that we are being judged by our spirits, but it does mean they are watching us!

Spirits stand on the side of the mirror that allows them to observe clearly! They can see us, hear us, and often spend many hours simply watching us. While this seems like an advantageous viewpoint, it can be frustrating for the spirits of our Beloved Dead, particularly if they are watching the ones they love suffer or make one stupid decision after another. Spirits spend a lot of time looking into the world of the living not simply so they can supervise the actions of the living, but because when we cross back across the veil into spirit, it is necessary for us to process the lives we just lived by witnessing how our actions affected not only our lives but the lives of those around us. Seeing into the world of the living while in spirit is important to our growth, although it can also be argued that the living are here to experience this world of solid form and therefore need to have some separation from the greater consciousness of spirit.

However, all this observation also means that spirits are often able to communicate about the current affairs in the lives of their living loved ones. As a medium I commonly experience spirits telling me about events that have recently happened in the lives of their loved ones, such as changes in their home, new relationships, hardships, and even conversations their loved ones had in the car on the way to their appointment with me.

On the opposite side of the mirror, the living have far more obstacles when it comes to communication. From the side of the living, the ability to hear and see through the "mirror," or the veil between the worlds, is limited. Often there is a feeling of being watched, but it is likely that only fleeting glimpses of what lies on the side of spirit will be caught by the living eye.

Mediums are like the cops who go between the rooms passing messages. They have developed an ability to sense the world of spirit more fully. That being said, the medium is still observed more clearly by the dead than the dead are by the medium. This is simply the way of the veil; it is more transparent from one side than the other.

🌿Becoming Aware of Spirit

There are techniques that you can develop to sharpen your awareness of the world of spirit, but like all things this takes time and dedication. If you are looking to do this, it is helpful to utilize wide-angle vision (see page 27), focusing your attention on the peripheral view, so as not to look through the spirit. It is also important to remember that not all spirit communication comes in the form of seeing. If you are feeling the spirit of your loved one with you, acknowledge it, celebrate it, and keep working on it! In the analogy of the two-way police mirror, imagine that you have a mental button that allows you to lower the reflective surface for a moment, giving you a glimpse of what's on the other side. Enhance your experience by imagining that images can come through to you in quick flashes of information when the mirror is temporarily down. It may also be useful to sit with a real mirror while practicing this exercise. You can do this by placing a small mirror on your ancestor altar and sitting in front of it by candlelight.

EMOTIONAL VOLUME

One of the most notable changes made to our perception upon death is the lowering of our emotional volume. This is an important factor that allows us to find peace in death and the ability to look at our life with more clarity, perceiving situations from multiple points of view, not just our own. In many ways it is like we get the backstory that explains how this led to that, not just from our own perspective but from the viewpoint of those who cared for us or caused us pain as well. We are able to understand the true nature of our life this way, as our emotions are turned down so that we can review our situation more analytically.

I often describe emotional volume through the analogy of a volume dial on a stereo. In this analogy the volume ranges from one to ten. Most people go through their life with their emotional volume set at around a three or a four, allowing their emotions to contribute to the background of their life without overwhelming it. Those who suffer with anxiety and depression often experience their emotional volume as more of an eight or a nine, meaning that it is often overpowering other experiences in their life, feeling all encompassing. Those who experience their emotional volume at such a high level often feel life to be unbearable and find themselves desperately seeking ways to bring their emotions into a range that will allow them to do more than just survive. When we die our emotional volume is turned down to about a two, allowing us to review our life more like we are watching television rather than as if it is happening directly to us.

This lack of emotional potency is one of the things that draws random spirits to mediums, for being around a medium connects a spirit more clearly to this world, which turns up that emotional volume and their ability to feel alive! This is why it is recommended that people wait a few months or even years before seeking communication with a spirit who died in a traumatic way, such as by suicide, overdose, or murder, and why it is unadvisable for an untrained medium to seek communication with such a spirit. Not because they are dangerous, but because there are generally deep, heavy emotions to be processed in such deaths, and the spirit may or may not be ready to face their living loved ones with such a high level of emotion. They not only experience their own emotions at a higher volume but those of their loved ones as well. This does not mean the spirit does not love their family but more that they may not be ready to sit in such emotional turmoil.

I stopped crying for the living during spirit communication settings a long time ago, but on occasion I do find myself tearing up for the dead, as sometimes they are so filled with emotion while sitting with me that I can't help but feel it. In these moments I share with my living clients the level of emotion I am feeling in connection to their Beloved Dead and how much they are loved and missed. I do this because I truly feel it! Just as I know how it feels to be in love with someone through the eyes of their partner, I also know how it feels to look upon the living loved ones of the spirit I sit with and feel the sorrow of that loss as if it were my own.

Sometimes I think it would be nice to be able to adjust our emotional volume. How much clarity would we have if we could use our emotions as spices we add to life, instead of allowing them to be the whole soup pot. But then I think of how many wonders and miracles have come about because of the level of emotion we are able to experience while living, and I see why they are so necessary. That being said, it would be nice if we could figure out a way to energetically turn down the volume for those who suffer oppressively with the drowning power of their emotions.

Through this experience of altered emotional input we are able to learn and grow as spirits. This often means that, given a bit of time, those who have suffered deep hardship in life and/or traumatic deaths can heal, and those whose emotions overwhelmed them in life can find clarity and understanding about how things went wrong along their path. As a medium I often see this play out in the form of the best version of a spirit showing up to communicate with their living loved ones. Having been able to think clearly, they are able to stand in their center.

TIME OUT

While death comes to us all, it does not always do so fairly. Ideally, we will die in our sleep at a ripe old age, after a fulfilling life, surrounded by our loved ones. But in truth, that is a blessing experienced by few. Many of us will find we have not processed our shit when death comes knocking, and for a few of us the circumstances surrounding our death will be traumatic, leaving those who love us distraught over what will become of our soul.

I would like to start by saying that I have never met a spirit who had been exiled to hell, nor have I met a spirit who claimed to have crossed the pearly gates of heaven. I am not saying there is no such thing as heaven or hell, but I believe it is not as straightforward as we might think. In fact, most spirits I speak to have memories of other lifetimes and speak about the healing and growth of their soul. This includes those who have passed into spirit in peril. With this multilife perspective of our soul, we have all experienced lifetimes that were too much for us to handle. We either died with things left unprocessed or through the violent actions of ourselves or others.

In the beginning of my work as a professional medium, I was advised by my spirit team to avoid contact with spirits who had died through acts of violence. At first I believed this was for my own safety, that such spirits might somehow be drawn to my light and seek to attach themselves to me. As my ability grew, and I asked more questions of my team and the spirits with whom I came in contact, I discovered that this was not advised for my safety but rather for the safety of the spirit involved. Understanding how the emotional volume dial works, I was able to see how a spirit who was still deeply in their trauma would be adversely affected by having their emotional dial turned back up to max, and with experience I learned how to gauge whether a spirit had healed enough to make such contact.

When someone dies suddenly and unexpectedly there is always a need to process the events in a controlled environment. I refer to this place as "Time Out," as it reminds me of putting a child in time out when they act up. The amount of time a soul needs to stay in this controlled environment greatly depends on the circumstances: the amount of time someone who had a sudden heart attack needs to spend there is significantly less than someone who died in an accident, through self-harm, or through acts of violence. It is not a place of punishment but more of a mandatory time of stepping away from the world so we can process the events surrounding our death. In addition to the manner of death, the amount of time a soul needs to spend in Time Out also depends on the soul itself and its ability to process. Remember, though, that emotions are greatly turned down in death, making this processing so much easier. In Time Out our contact with others is limited to those who are holding space as guides for us, making sure that we follow through on our contemplation, as we don't get out of the seat until we do! Again, this is not a place of punishment but one of reflection.

For those who die at their own hands—both intentionally through suicide and haphazardly through drug overdose or an accident in which the person's death was due to repetitive reckless behavior—there is a variety of emotions carried over from life, and most likely a series of unprocessed abuses too heavy for them to handle while living. In such cases the person was most likely already experiencing a form of hell in life, their emotional traumas drowning them a bit more every day. People do not make decisions to harm themselves lightly. Instead they come to it a bit at a time, caving to the pressure of their wounding. While I do not condone self-harm, I also make a point of understanding where it comes from. My experience with the dead confirms my belief that the universe is not unkind. Souls who suffer so are not punished but instead put into Time Out, a place of deep healing meant to give them an opportunity to unravel the traumas that bind them, and heal.

If a person dies violently through the hands of another, they may also need to sit in Time Out while they move through the trauma of their death. In such cases I find the wisdom and experience of the soul plays a big part in how long it takes to rationalize the situation. Years ago, a local school teacher in my area was brutally murdered. As she was an acquaintance of mine, having frequented the bar I owned while she was in college, she appeared to me within days of her death, and I knew I would help her family in some way to process her death. Within a month of her passing, I met with multiple members of her family, and every time she came through, I was blown away by how little damage her soul had taken. While her experience had been traumatic, her soul had suffered little permanent damage. Instead, she stood boldly, a month after her murder, speaking of the needs of her child, trying desperately to mother from the other side. Her sit in Time Out had been a short one! On the flip side of that, I did a spirit communication connecting a man in his fifties to his mother, who had died when he was in his twenties at the hand of his brother. She was shot by her son while he was mentally spiraling and strung out on drugs, before he shot and killed himself. This was such a traumatizing act that the mother's soul was still processing the event thirty years later, her need for a selective environment still strong.

I have developed my skill as a medium to understand when a spirit needs adaptive communication, which means they communicate through my spirit guide Adam, who in turn communicates with me. This is something I commonly practice when connecting with spirits who are still in Time Out. In this way I can control the volume adjustment that comes when a spirit connects with a medium. If you are looking to connect with a loved one who you believe may be in Time Out, it is helpful to ask another close spirit to work between you. It is also important to understand when a medium tells you that soul is not yet ready for communication or that they are unable to speak of certain things, like the exact cause of their death.

We can end up in Time Out even if we die of natural causes at a ripe old age. Living a life of deceit, malice, or self-abuse may also require us to spend some time in the healing environment of seclusion. This is a way of making sure we look at those things we would rather avoid, like the pain we have caused others. There is forgiveness for even the darkest of souls, but the forgiveness does not come from God or the ones we harmed but rather from ourselves. It is a hard-earned thing that involves dissecting the misdeeds of our life and seeing how our own unprocessed traumas created the violence we turned on others. When the lessons are finally learned in the spirit world, it is then time for us to learn the lessons in the physical, meaning our next life will likely provide us the means to learn directly from our actions.

7

HEALING THE DEAD

WHEN A PERSON DIES either at the hands of another or by their own hand, whether it was intentional, accidental, or impulsive as is the case of some suicides, it is a traumatic death. Such situations cause great pain for those who are left behind and who often spend countless hours torturing themselves with all the things they should have said and done and all the ways God and the universe are unfair. Somewhere in this suffering it is likely that fear for the soul of their loved one enters the minds of those who are mourning, coming from deep within their subconscious, where it was first created by religious doctrine and cultural beliefs most of us have outgrown.

Those who experience traumatic deaths, such as murders, suicides, and overdoses, are often confused when they cross into spirit, as the violence has shaken them up. Most often they stay close to their body until it is discovered, or until the Wisdom Keeper of their family comes to get them. Even in cases where the body is never recovered, the spirit may stay connected to their body in the hope that others will find peace through finding their remains. However, in most of these cases the spirit is not stuck there; it chooses to remain.

As discussed in the previous chapter, emotions are high for those who experience traumatic deaths. When those deaths are due to the violent acts of others, the emotions surrounding the situation vary in accordance with how personal the violence was and how wise the victim was. If the victim was not personally targeted, there may be little soul-level damage, but there is generally a lot of confusion for the newly dead in such cases as they try to understand what has happened to them. Those whose death was premeditated and/or forewarned through threats or previous violence often have a lot of emotions to process out.

Those who die due to their own actions have often lived long with their pain and fear. Struggling with mental illness, addiction, or abuse, they have already experienced a form of hell in life, making death in many ways a relief, as they are finally able to surface from the emotions that had overwhelmed them and drowned out all rational thought like a stereo set on full volume, day in and day out. However, these souls end up in Time Out (see chapter 6) after they pass, and while the experiences vary depending on one's reason for being there, all troubled souls go through a more controlled version of crossing into spirit. They are still greeted by the spiritual elder of the ancestors and/or someone who loved them dearly, but their interaction with the spirit world and their greater spirit family is more controlled, and their ability to interact with the living is restricted in accordance with how heavy their emotional baggage is.

In the past several years, I have seen a great increase in the number of spirits I connect with who were at least partially responsible for their own death, either by suicide, overdose, or reckless behavior. In casually tracking this increase, I have also noticed that many of the spirits who are crossing this way were not the victims of abuse or people who had significant mental illness in their life. It used to be that spirits I met who were responsible for their own death were deeply troubled, often suffering with emotional trauma that led to their self-abuse. Now it is not uncommon to encounter spirits who simply took a wrong turn, developing a drug addiction after being prescribed pain medication or overdosing on high-potency drugs like fentanyl when they thought they had things under control.

These deaths fall somewhere between an accident and suicide, which is why these souls are considered at least partially responsible for their own death. In the case of such deaths, the way their family responds will greatly influence how long it takes the soul to move on from the limbo state of Time Out. When their family approaches their death with purpose, seeking to understand and educate themselves and others around the cause of death, the spirit seems to heal rapidly.

The effect is similar for spirits who lost their lives violently through the actions of others. In these cases, how the family heals greatly affects the spirit's healing. By no means am I suggesting that people forgo mourning, as it is a deeply important part of the death experience. Instead I am showing how interconnected we are with our dead. We need to mourn, for doing so is necessary to our healing, but we also need to reemerge into life again, find purpose, and continue along our path. When we get stuck in our pain, we do not exist there alone. Our Beloved Dead are tuned in to the channel that plays out our pain regularly, which is why some spirits stay in Time Out until the loved ones who mourn them must also cross into spirit.

ALTARS FOR HEALING

It's hard to simply let go of our pain, yet knowing our healing is important for the healing of our Beloved Dead, many of us will want to do so, but we have no idea where to start. I recommend creating an altar or shrine (see chapter 1) as a physical reminder that the work we do spiritually is helpful, particularly when it comes to healing the dead. While I have focused on traumatic deaths here, healing altars need not be limited to spirits who died violently, they are also a great idea for our Beloved Dead who struggled in life, with feelings of inadequacy, low-level depression, long-term illness, and more. In fact, I recommend creating an altar for anyone you loved, especially those who were not prepared and ready for death when it came for them. The exercise below provides instructions for doing so.

🌿Creating a Healing Altar for Your Beloved Dead

All ancestor altars are healing altars. They are spaces we create to connect with our Beloved Dead so that we may know that they are still with us; places to seek council, speaking to those who gave us peace; and places of healing for ourselves and the dead we love. I encourage you to set up an ancestor altar in a permanent location and to interact with it regularly. Below is an example of a personal shrine, created for an individual soul who experienced trauma around their death. Feel free to adapt it to your needs.

You will need a photo(s) of your Beloved Dead showing them when they were happy and healthy; memorabilia of their life and journey; something that represents their struggle, such as a beer can or a poem written during a time of darkness; a gift box big enough to hold the symbol of their struggle; and a tealight to represent the light you shine into the spirit world.

1. Start by setting up your altar in a way that looks and feels pleasing to you, allowing yourself to create it in a fashion you believe your Beloved Dead would enjoy.

2. Place the item of their struggle into a gift box and address it to your loved one. For example, *To my beloved son, for your transformation.* Know that you are handing them the means of transformation so they may learn from that which troubled them and never need to learn it again.

3. Light your tealight and send your light out into the spirit world, imagining it like a beacon to your Beloved Dead.

4. Begin speaking to your Beloved Dead, telling them how much you love them and miss them as you explain your goal of transforming that which troubled them into a power for healing. Focusing on the gift box, begin sending the light of your candle into the box, imagining you are fueling it with healing energy—energy that is your light. Speak about the lessons you have learned from this "gift"; although they may be painful and raw, these experiences are still lessons learned, and healing comes through transformation. By not hiding from the demons that haunted our Beloved Dead, we are taking away the power the demons hold.

5. Return to this altar on a regular basis, each time extending the light of your candle first to yourself, then to your Beloved Dead, and finally to the box of transformation.

6. Do this for thirty days, or as long as you feel moved to. When you feel the work is complete, remove the item from the box, disposing of it properly (garbage, recycling, etc.), and continue to work with the box, this time filling it with the dreams you wish for your Beloved Dead, items that represent healing and growth.

Regardless of how you approach healing, know that healing yourself is important to the healing of your Beloved Dead, for your pain affects them greatly!

ANCESTRAL HEALING

I grew up with my father's family, under the influence of Grammy Brown, who was the supreme matriarch of our tribe of misfits. Many of our traditions were kept secret due to the fact that my ancestors had experienced persecution because of their customs and simply for who they were. The silver lining of this protective shielding is that we never lost the traditions that allowed us to stay connected to our ancestors. Hiding how we honored and celebrated our Beloved Dead made these things precious, allowing me to develop my connection to spirit in a protective bubble of sorts, one in which I did not feel persecuted for believing as I did. As a child I did not see it as hidden; I simply saw it as how things were done.

My family has a strong connection to our Beloved Dead, something Grammy Brown had instilled in each of us, as she shared traditions of our Irish Traveler and Blackfoot roots. Regardless of whether we shared her gift of communicating with the dead, we all knew that our ancestors were around us and that they expected to be included in family gatherings—most often through storytelling. As one of the ones who carried psychic gifts, I understood why it was important for us to include them, as I could feel and see my ancestors whenever a group of us gathered in celebration or sorrow. I knew they were thankful for being included, and I believed Grammy when she said they were watching over us, as I could see them myself!

Grammy often talked about the paths her ancestors had taken and the hardships they faced. I knew my people had truly struggled with poverty and persecution, but I also knew they were people of song, story, magic, and the Earth. Often after people came to visit Grammy for her good cooking or to buy some worms, using either one as a guise for sitting with my great-grandmother to talk with their dead or have her look into their future, she would sit down with me and ask me what I thought, knowing I could see things not only about the people but the souls who had come with them as well. She would explain that the problems carried by a person may be handed down, like a curse of sorts, and so often the man who struggled to quit drinking was doing so not only for himself but also for the line of ancestors who carried the same burden for generations. Grammy also said that one of the challenges we face in life is believing that our problems are ours alone!

Many of us understand what it means to carry on the burden of family wounding, as we experience generational psychosis, addiction, and abuse. We see how the actions of the parent influence the child, who then in turn does the same thing, and chances are those of you who are reading this are the ones who want to put an end to the cycle! Just as we can send healing to our loved ones who have died traumatically, we can send healing to our ancestors and begin the work of breaking patterns and healing generational wounding. In fact, I believe many of us are here in this lifetime for that very purpose: to heal our family lines and create new pathways in which we can flourish. This is not done with altars alone but by looking deeply at the wounding and tracing it back through the bloodline, seeing why the father who was cold and harsh became so and why his mother before him did the things she did. By tracing the steps, we can see where things went wrong, and in truth you don't really have to go that far back to begin the healing.

When working on healing dysfunctional patterns in our family line we first need to start with ourselves, taking a good look at who we are and how we got to be so. What traumas did we experience at the hands of our family? What patterns that do not serve us came through the influence of another? What troubles seem to plague your family as a whole? Does your family struggle with addiction, emotional manipulation, self-destructive behavior, or generational mental illness? Just as physical issues can be passed down through the generations, so, too, can behaviors. Knowing who and what we are and where we come from allows us not only to heal ourselves but also to create alternative pathways for future generations, showing them that we can choose another way. It also allows the spirits of our ancestors to heal.

Often when we take on the role of healer for our family line, we are not doing so alone. On the other side of the veil, we will find allies, family members who, like us, want to see an end to the destructive behaviors. Interestingly enough, it is often the ancestor who played a significant part in creating the malfunctioning pattern who steps up for the job, for they have had to watch for generations as their damage continued to play out. The great-great-grandfather who beat his wife and children after experiencing the violence and pain of war watched his children continuing the pattern of abuse with their families, and then their children doing the same. In the beginning, when such things occur, they know not the level of destruction that will follow in their wake, and as they watch from the vantage point of spirit the generational story they have created, they are hopeful that someone will come along who can help shift the pattern.

It's important when we are looking at our own damage to see where it came from. My father was a disabled marine who lost his eye in Vietnam. Abandoned by his parents, he grew up living with his grandmother and brothers on the edge of poverty. Having trau-matic brain damage from injuries received in Vietnam and coming from a line of alcoholics, it was not surprising that my father, too, became an alcoholic. When Grammy Brown died, he lost the only person who anchored him as she was both mother and grandmother to him, his alcoholism spiraled out of control, and through his actions he lost his wife and children.

I did not speak to my father for thirteen years, during which time he became sober, and we both did a lot of healing. In the end it was the spirits—particularly Grammy Brown—who reconnected us. Grammy came to me every night, speaking to me in my mind, telling me about horrific things and then saying, "Did that happen to you, Sali?" When I replied, "No!" she would say, "Huh, well that did happen to your father. I am surprised he didn't do that to you," making a point of showing me how my father had done the best he knew how considering the life he had experienced. This helped me to see that while my father had been verbally abusive, he had restrained himself and not carried on the level of damage he had experienced. While it did not excuse his actions, it helped me to understand the way trauma moves through families, either picking up steam or becoming diminished generation by generation. Through Grammy Brown's help, my father and I were able to heal our relationship, and I have made it a big part of my life to continue healing our family's wounds of abuse, alcoholism, and abandonment.

If you are ready to step into the role of family healer, start with identifying the wounds your family has passed down and look at the reasons such things exist. Speak about them; don't leave them in the closet to fester. When we speak of such things, we shed light on them, and it is only through this light and bringing things out in the open that we can truly heal the larger family. Educate your children about your family's weakness. I spoke often to my children about our family's tendency toward addiction, telling them that just like some families have a higher risk of heart disease or diabetes, our family had a higher risk of addiction. This helped my children to make better decisions, as they truly knew the risk they ran. I have also seen myself as a role model to those in the family who needed to see another path. Through me they could see that not all of us were alcoholics, which gave even those not directly connected to me another option!

We need a place to center our prayers and healing efforts, and this is where your ancestor altar comes in again. Just as we can set up an altar to help heal our recently departed loved ones, we can expand our altar to include photos and memorabilia of the ancestors who came before us. If we are seeking to heal a line of abuse, we need to acknowledge the abusers as much as the healers, for the abusers have most likely been abused themselves. I learned this first-hand when I became a Reiki master. In my zest to become a healer I put it out to the universe that I wanted to heal the victims. To my surprise the first year of my practice was filled with people struggling with addiction. This showed me not only important aspects of my own story but also things I felt could be true for us all. I found that those who victimize others must be healed, as they are first and foremost victims themselves, their actions the result of their wounding. With that in mind you will see how they, too, deserve space on the ancestor altar, and by providing it we make a true change in our family line.

LIVING WITH OUR BELOVED DEAD

I am a person who lives with my dead. They are woven into my daily life and hold just as much space in my heart and mind as the living. I am who I am because they came before me, teaching me with their kindness as well as with the wounds they inflicted. None of us is perfect; we are all growing, changing, and becoming. Just as we inevitably realize our parents did not have it all figured out, we, too, need to understand that our ancestors experienced their own tragedies, wounding, and growth. They are allies on our path to becoming, and by giving regular offerings, the relationship between us and our dead is strengthened. As we do so we heal ourselves and those who are part of our family line.

Living with our Beloved Dead, continuing relationships far beyond the grave, gives us a feeling of wholeness. Over time we will find that our offerings and altar interactions help us to become more sensitive to the coming and going of spirits, and our ability to feel, smell, and know will be heightened. Regardless of whether we are highly sensitive, natural mediums, or feel blocked from the world of spirit, this regular interaction will change us, opening us to the unseen world in a gentle, comforting way.

It is my hope that in reading this book you are filled with the desire to have a closer relationship with your Beloved Dead, for when we expand our consciousness to include the unseen world, we begin to see the value of those who have gone before us, as well as the effect we have on those who follow in our ancestral line. This influence not only affects those who follow our direct ancestry, it also weaves itself into the most unusual of places. Children of cousins we have never met may be inspired by your kindness, bravery, and talent. The great-grandchildren of our siblings may see us as the role model for their own healing or choice of career.

Most of us are fascinated by who we are and where we come from, sending in our saliva to the AncestryDNA site in the hope of understanding the genetic markers that make up our being and searching the archives of Ancestry.com for unknown relatives. We do this because it matters. We do this because our strands of fate are part of the same tapestry.

I was recently contacted by one of my cousins in Maryland, who told me that her daughter had just bought a book on crystals because she wanted to be like her cousin Sali when she grew up. A perfect example of how we can influence someone we don't even know. While her mother was one of my closer cousins, we saw each other for only a couple of days each year, when visiting my mother's family, and stopped entirely when I became an adult. Yet for a person wanting to develop their intuitive gifts, finding a relative with developed skill in the field is inspiring, giving them something to relate to.

I have seen this time and time again with my students, how excited they get when they share stories of having a grandmother or great aunt who read tea leaves or saw spirits. Such talents give recognition to the fact that certain skills belong in our family. The same is true of soldiers who connect with their great-grandfather who fought in World War II or musicians who are excited to know their great-great-uncle played at the Grand Ole Opry. We know inside ourselves that we are woven together, even if we don't all touch directly. I think this is the reason Grammy Brown made such a big deal about us knowing of our dead family members; they are part of the great pattern we are connected to.

Many of us will feel more connected to some parts of our ancestry than others. As a psychic medium I feel most connected to the "magical" line of my family, particularly the Irish Traveler side. This bloodline sings to me, back through my father and my father's father to my father's father's mother—Grammy Brown—and her father, William Thomas, who was an Irish Traveler or Tinker, sometimes also known as an Irish Gypsy. William Thomas left Ireland with his brother, crossing the Atlantic to make a better life for himself. He first landed in Canada, becoming a Mountie for a short while before marrying a Blackfoot bride, my great-great-grandmother Little Beaver. When I was doing séances in people's homes, traveling within an hour-and-a-half radius of my home three times a week to communicate with people's dead, I could feel William Thomas. I could see how my traveling around, peddling my psychic abilities, was similar to the life of a Traveler. I knew it made him proud to see his great-great-granddaughter following his ancestral path.

Do you favor one side of the family more than another? Is there someone in your family ancestry who fascinates you? Do you look remarkably similar to a distant relative? Do you have an unusual personality trait or skill that someone else in the family shares?

Remembering that spirits have a tendency to reincarnate into their family or tribal lines helps us to understand the connections we feel to relatives we have never met in this lifetime. It also explains how we can feel closer to particular ancestral lines. Some time ago, during a psilocybin journey, I decided to look at my bloodlines and how they affected me. Having done a previous journey years before in which I looked at my DNA, I wanted to see how my mother's line played into mine, as my father's line, particularly the Traveler's line, was so dominant in my life. In the experience I viewed the bloodlines like waterways. My father's line was like a rushing river, moving fast with high water. My mother's line was like a trickling stream that got swallowed up when it met with the blood of my father, adding to the river but not changing the course.

While a few will feel equally connected to all of their ancestry, most will relate to my story. My great-grandmother would say it was because that part of our bloodline was singing to us, meaning it was activated! Siblings raised within the same family and same traditions can feel a stronger connection to opposite sides of the family, because their blood is singing different tunes. My sister Sandy, while still feeling connected to Grammy Brown's line, is more influenced by the Blackfoot blood carried through our great-great-grandmother Little Beaver/Cora.

Living with our dead means keeping their stories alive. Like Grammy Brown, I have shared stories of my Beloved Dead with my children and grandchildren. I don't wait for special occasions; instead, I talk about them all the time. Cooking dinner is the perfect time for talking about how my great-grandmother never used recipes and cooked off a wood cookstove until she was in her late seventies. Walking in the woods or starting a campfire allows me to talk about my own childhood and how my father, a marine who did recon in Vietnam, was always teaching us survival tips. While we don't have to wait for special occasions, holidays do give us ample opportunity to talk about our extended family, the great aunts and uncles of our childhood.

One of my favorite things to do on holidays, something much appreciated by the dead, is to set a plate for spirit at the festivities. It's an easy thing to do, and it creates the perfect opportunity for honoring our Beloved Dead. Simply place a plate on the ancestor altar and invite people to place the favorite foods of their loved ones in spirit on it throughout the day. When giving an offering, a story must also be told of the ancestor being honored. In some traditions the food on the plate is seen as being for the spirits alone and must be thrown away or composted. But as I have said, my traditions come from poor, Traveler stock; we don't waste food! Instead, we eat it. When the plate is full, we reverse the process, and people can pick things off the ancestor's plate, once again paying the price of a story to do so.

Living with our dead means making space for them, including them in our family gatherings and daily life. In doing so we not only heal the grief of loss, we begin to develop a sensitivity to the spirit world as well. While not all of us will hear the voices of spirits or see them with our eyes or in our minds, we all will feel them in our heart. This is not a new thing but a return to the old ways, ways that recognized the eternal spirit and the connection between those who share bloodlines and bonds of friendship.

May your hearts be full and your spirit open. May you build strong bonds of healing and protection within the tapestry of your ancestry. May we all become more aware of the unseen world that we may grow as a species into more conscious beings!

SPREADING LOVE,
SALICROW

INDEX

"Awareness" by Robin Lee Wedemeyer